KU-499-910

*General Editor:*
*Patrick McNeill*

**SOCIETY**
**NOW**

*Health*

*Peter Aggleton*

# HEALTH

London and New York

First published 1990

Reprinted 1991, 1992, 1993, 1994, 1995
by Routledge
11 New Fetter Lane, London EC4P 4EE

Simultaneously published in the USA and Canada
by Routledge
29 West 35th Street, New York, NY 10001

© 1990 Peter Aggleton

Typeset in Times by J & L Composition Ltd, Filey, North Yorkshire
Printed and bound in Great Britain by Cox & Wyman Ltd, Reading, Ber

All rights reserved. No part of this book may be reprinted or reproduced
or utilized in any form or by any electronic, mechanical, or other means,
now known or hereafter invented, including photocopying and recording
or in any information storage or retrieval system, without permission in
writing from the publishers.

*British Library Cataloguing in Publication Data*
A catalogue record for this book is available from the British Library

ISBN 0–415–00816–6

# Contents

# Illustrations

*Tables*

# Preface

There are many books on health, disease, and illness written from a biological or medical perspective. These provide some insight into the issues, but tend to marginalize the social factors affecting health and well-being. They also contain little guidance on how to make sense of different patterns of health care provision. This book offers an introduction to some of the alternative accounts of these processes developed by sociologists and other social researchers. It has been written with three audiences in mind – those requiring an introduction to the sociology of health and illness; those undertaking introductory courses in medical sociology; and those, such as nurses and health visitors, who are likely to encounter sociological ideas as part of their education and training.

Many people have inspired and supported me over the past twelve years. To Helen Chalmers, who encouraged my efforts to make sociological ideas relevant to health professionals, I owe a special debt. To Meurig Horton and Simon Watney, I am grateful for constant reminders that the analysis of health, illness, and disease is, and must always be, a political issue. To Ian Warwick, I am grateful for his personal support and his critical reading of parts of this book. And to Len Barton, Helen Thomas, Marilyn Toft, Stuart Watson, and Geoff Whitty I am grateful for their friendship, humour, and commitment in these difficult times. Finally, I must thank Andy, without whose love, support, and understanding this book could never have been written.

Peter Aggleton

# 1

# *Defining health*

There are many words that we think we understand until we begin to question what they mean. 'Health' is one of them. At first sight, the word looks quite straightforward. It identifies a state of being to which most of us aspire – a 'blessing', a desirable quality, but one which we are often told money cannot buy. But if we pause for a moment to think just what health is, the picture becomes more complicated.

For the sports enthusiast, health may be equated with physical fitness: the ability to finish a race in a certain time, or the ability to swim so many lengths of the pool. For others, health may be the feeling of contentment that comes from less active pursuits such as cultivating a sun tan while lying on the beach. For many of those who are young, health may be associated with participation in a variety of activities, whereas for many people over 75, health may be the ability to undertake a more restricted range of actions, such as being able to get out to the local shops every day. For some, it may be healthy to begin the day with a hefty breakfast of bacon, eggs, and fried bread. For others, muesli and home-made yoghurt may suffice. For yet other people, an early morning run followed by a cup of black coffee, and that alone, may be seen as the best way to begin the day. Clearly there is little consensus about what health is: at least when defined in these terms, still less is there agreement about the means by which it can be achieved.

The situation is further complicated by the fact that some people may be healthy according to some criteria but not others. Consider for example the case of sports enthusiasts who are highly skilled in their favourite team sport but who consume five pints of lager after every match – are they healthy or not? Think about well-adjusted, happy and outward-going chefs who happen to weigh 17 stone – are they healthy or not? Think for a moment about well-liked and reasonably content teachers who smoke thirty cigarettes a day in order to cope with their job – are they healthy or not? And what about people who are the life and soul of the party but who curl up in bed and cry themselves to sleep every night – are they healthy or not?

These examples raise important questions about the difference between physical and mental health – the ability to carry out a range of physical activities and the ability to cope psychologically with the demands of everyday life. While this book will not specifically focus on mental health, except in so far as it has the potential to inform our appreciation of the social dimensions of health, it is important to recognize from the start that health is a multifaceted phenomenon.

## Activities

1 Try to decide which of the following six people is physically healthy and which is mentally healthy. Give each person a rating from 1 to 5 on each of these qualities. 1 is very unhealthy and 5 is very healthy. Make a record of your personal decisions.

2 Discuss your feelings with others and try to reach a consensus or agreement about each person. Why is it hard to agree about some of the people described?

- Brenda works in an office and enjoys going out dancing with her girlfriends. She also likes to diet and has lost two and a half stone over the past six months. She is really pleased that she now weighs six and a half stone.
- Paul is a 50-year-old farmer. He enjoys working out of doors, especially in the summer. Last year he discovered that several of the freckles on his arms had started to itch and grow in size. They now bleed when he scratches them. He is not worried about this and carries on as normal.
- Suzie is 36 and owns a small antiques shop. Every lunchtime she likes to go to the local pub along with a couple of friends in the antiques trade. Between them they manage to consume two or three bottles of red wine.
- Steve works as a mechanic in a garage. He considers himself fit, plays football at weekends, and trains once a week. Every season, he seems to run into problems. This time it's his knee which is playing him up. As a result, he has had to take a few weeks off work.
- Wendy is 24 with two young children. She rarely goes out except to do the shopping and spends much of her time watching television. She enjoys the crisps, soft drinks, and savoury snacks that are always to hand when the television is on.
- Kevin is a committed Christian. He prays four times a day and attends church twice on Sundays. He thinks that AIDS is God's revenge on perverts and promiscuous people.

Given what has been said so far, it is going to be important for us to develop our understanding of health more fully so that we can identify some of the different ways in which the term is used.

## Defining terms

Social scientists, like most people, need to reach some consensus about what words mean if they are to communicate effectively with one another. They do this because the terms they use – words such as family, class, gender, race, age, mobility, crime, deviance, health – are the concepts or building blocks out of which more substantial theories are constructed.

There are many ways of defining health, but generally speaking these can be divided into two broad types. First, there are what we can call *official definitions* – the views of doctors and other health professionals. Then there are more popular perceptions of health – the views of those who are not professionally involved in health issues. These *lay beliefs* about health, as they are sometimes called, are no less important than official definitions, since they influence the ways in which people understand and respond to health issues. They co-exist alongside official views about health, and they even inform the actions of doctors, nurses, health visitors, and health education officers.

Beliefs about health vary from place to place as well as at different times in history. For example, health may be perceived very differently in a community in which many children die within the first year of life and in which adult life expectancy is low, than in a situation in which everyone is well-fed and where adults live into their 60s and 70s. Similarly there are those for whom the term health currently conjures up visions of jacuzzis, saunas, health farms, and designer tracksuits – imagery that would have been unthinkable fifty years ago, and imagery that may be similarly unthinkable in fifty years' time. Health is therefore a relative quality – relative that is to the surroundings and circumstances in which people find themselves.

Arthur Kleinman (1980) has offered a framework which goes some way to explaining the existence of these competing views about health. He distinguishes between three environments, or *arenas*, in which healing can take place: the popular arena, the folk arena, and the professional arena. The first of these is often the home or community within which we live. The second arena is the one in which non-professional healing specialists – such as clairvoyants, faith healers, and herbalists – operate. The third arena is made up of modern professional bio-medicine as well as what Kleinman calls the professionalized healing traditions of Indian, Chinese, and native American medicine.

Each of these three arenas gives rise to a particular set of health practices and activities. Modern bio-medicine, for example, emphasizes the value of drug therapy and, in appropriate circumstances, surgery. Similarly at home, emphasis may be placed on the value of hot drinks and keeping warm as treatment for health complaints. Associated with the health practices of each arena are ways of under-standing health and health issues, which make the actions taken in it seem sensible and logical. These beliefs about health circulate within each of the three arenas, but occasion-ally cross over from one arena to another. For example, the belief that colds are caused by failing to wrap up well in winter (a widespread view in the popular arena in Britain and North America today) may also inform the actions of doctors and other health professionals. This, and not the logic of the professional arena, may encourage them to advise their clients to wear a warm overcoat when going out in winter.

## Official definitions of health

Official definitions of health are of two main types. First, there are those which define health negatively, as the absence of certain qualities such as disease and illness. Second, there are those which adopt a more positive stance. We need to consider both of these kinds of definitions if we are to develop a comprehensive understanding of what health is.

## Negative definitions

There are two main ways of seeing health negatively. The first equates it with the absence of disease or bodily abnormality, the second with the absence of illness or the feelings of anxiety, pain, or distress that may or may not accompany disease.

*Disease* is usually understood as the presence of some pathology or abnormality in a part of the body. Bacteria and viruses cause many diseases. Measles and smallpox are diseases. Cancer is a disease. With the advent of modern bio-medicine (medicine founded on biological principles), this way of understanding health has become particularly widespread.

It is important to recognize, however, that diseases may or may not be accompanied by feelings of anxiety or distress. Some people may be diseased without even knowing it: this is often the case with minor infections. On other occasions, it may be some time before an abnormality or disturbance in the body's functioning makes its presence known. For example, someone's teeth may have been decaying for some time before they experience pain and visit the dentist.

David Field (1976) has drawn an important distinction between the kinds of abnormalities that signal disease and the feelings that individuals have about themselves. When the latter take the form of pain or discomfort, the person is said to be ill. *Illness* is therefore a subjective experience, and one, moreover, that may or may not accompany disease.

Often subjective feelings of distress do accompany disease. Think back to the last time you had a cold: did you feel excited or happy about it? Or did you feel tired and depressed? On other occasions, however, people can feel ill in situations where doctors may be quite unable to detect any underlying pathology. In these circumstances, they may be accused of malingering or perhaps of being neurotic. However, to be labelled thus may not make the subjective feelings of illness any the less intense. Indeed, it may actually increase them.

## Health as the absence of disease

According to one negative definition of health, people are healthy so long as they show no signs of bodily abnormality. This is the case regardless of how they feel about themselves.

A number of problems have been raised with this way of defining health. In particular, it has been suggested that the notion of abnormality or pathology implies that certain universal 'norms' exist against which an individual can be assessed when making the judgement whether they are healthy or not – 'norms' that is which relate to the way in which the body should function when it is healthy. Sally Macintyre (1986) has, however, questioned whether such standards actually exist. Her research points to wide variations in human anatomy and physiology. Furthermore, as we have seen, deviation from these 'norms' is not always accompanied by feelings of distress. This line of reasoning has led some social scientists to define health rather differently, as the absence of illness.

## Health as the absence of illness

Illness was earlier defined as a set of unpleasant feelings that may or may not accompany disease. In contrast to disease, which is generally diagnosed for us by a doctor or other expert, illness is something which is experienced. According to this definition, therefore, so long as someone does not experience anxiety, pain, or distress, they are healthy.

There are, however, some problems with defining health in these terms. First, the definition can be accused of *relativism* – of suggesting that health is a purely subjective experience. While it may be important to know about individuals' feelings about their health, there may be some experiences that are common to particular social groups. Elderly people, for example, may have different health expectations from those who are young, as may those who live in poverty compared with those who live more affluently (Blaxter and Paterson

7

1982). A second problem with the definition stems from the fact that it allows us to define health only after the event. That is, we know whether someone is healthy or not only after they have reported feelings of well-being or illness. This may not be particularly helpful if we are planning to help people avoid ill-health in the first place.

## Positive definitions

In a recent book, David Seedhouse (1986) has distinguished between a number of different ways of defining health in positive terms. All of these suggest that health can be characterized by the presence of certain qualities. Five of these approaches are seen as particularly important.

## Health as an ideal state

In 1946 the World Health Organisation (WHO) defined health in a way very different from any of the definitions so far considered. It defined it as 'a state of complete physical, mental and social well-being and not merely the absence of disease or infirmity' (WHO 1946). While this kind of definition sets high targets to be achieved, it has been criticized for its idealism, for specifying a state of being which it is impossible to attain. It also puts forward a rather absolute view of health by suggesting that we are all unhealthy unless we have attained complete physical, mental, and social well-being.

---

**Activities**

1 Make a list of the qualities you would expect someone to display if they were
  • physically healthy
  • mentally healthy
  • socially healthy.

2 Discuss your list with others in groups of about four. Identify the features about which there is agreement as well as those about which you disagree. Why is it easier to reach agreement on some qualities than others?

---

Nevertheless, WHO's definition has acted as an impetus for other similar attempts to clarify the meaning of health. Linda Ewles and Ina Simnett (1985), for example, have added a further three dimensions to those specified in the World Health Organisation's statement. They suggest that there are emotional, spiritual, and societal aspects of health that also need to be considered. Other writers have suggested that a positive definition of health needs to consider some of the spiritual, sensual, and sexual dimensions of health. This kind of thinking encourages people to think of health more *holistically*, as something that relates to a wide range of human capacities and qualities (see Figure 1).

## Health as physical and mental fitness

In 1972 Talcott Parsons defined health as 'the state of optimum capacity of an individual for the effective performance of the roles and tasks for which (s)he has been socialized' (Parsons 1972: 117). This kind of definition, which emphasizes the capacity of an individual to 'fit in' with society's norms and expectations is sometimes described as a *normative* approach. It has its origins in Parsons's view that a high level of health is important for the smooth running of society. According to this perspective, too low a level of health, or too high a level of disease or illness, is likely to be dysfunctional for society and must therefore be kept in check.

Parsons's definition has been criticized for ignoring the existence of degrees of health. It defines health clearly as an 'optimum capacity'; anything other than this is obviously not health. The definition therefore fails to allow for the existence

Figure 1   *The dimensions of health – a holistic view*

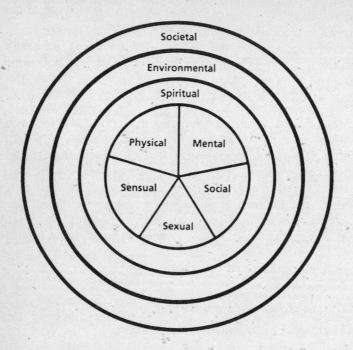

*Source*: Aggleton and Homans (1987)

of variations in health. It also implies that ill-health is something that is intrisically bad for society. In some circumstances this may be true, but as we will see later in Chapter 6, there may be occasions when ill-health can be a powerful force for social change and greater equality.

### Health as a commodity

The idea that health is a commodity is a modern one. David Seedhouse writes, 'The predominant image which overshadows medicine and the British health service is that health is a commodity. That it is something – albeit an amorphous thing – which can be supplied. Equally, it is something which can be lost' (Seedhouse 1986: 34). Ideas like these suggest that health is something which can be bought (by investment in private health care), sold (via health food stores and health centres), given (by surgery and drugs) and lost (following accident or disease). According to Oliver Sacks (1982), this way of seeing health is closely related to the growth of modern medicine, many of whose practices have claimed to be able to restore health in those who are sick.

There are a number of reasons why we should be sceptical of viewing health like this. First, this kind of approach seeks to equate health with a series of clearly definable and measurable qualities – things that can be readily obtained from others, moreover things that can be bought and sold. Second, it suggests that health is something that is in a sense removed from the person. Thus restoring an individual to health is little more than a technical matter – something to be performed by experts through the administration of drugs or by surgical intervention.

## Health as a personal strength or ability

Health can also be defined as a reserve of strength or energy. Sometimes the emphasis may be on the physical strength or the ability to resist disease and cope with illness. On other occasions, the emphasis may be on mental strength – an attitude or outlook on life which helps the individual cope with adversity. Finally, there can be the idea that health is the ability to adapt to changing circumstances. Rene Dubos (1959), for example, has suggested that it was the human capacity to adapt to new situations, and not the advent of vaccines and drugs, that resulted in the decline of epidemic disease in Europe in the nineteenth and twentieth centuries.

While these kinds of views are widely held, they are rather vague. For example, the nature of the personal strengths and abilities that make up health is rarely defined by those who

11

subscribe to ideas like these. Similarly little guidance is given on how these strengths and abilities can be measured other than in terms of the reports that individuals give of them. Nor is much said about the origins of these capacities, or the ways in which they might be acquired by those who presently lack them.

## Health as the basis for personal potential

A fifth way of defining health, and one which David Seedhouse favours, is to suggest that health is made up of a number of factors which help people to achieve their maximum personal potential. Seedhouse calls these factors *foundations for achievement*. Some are common to all, whereas others may be unique to the individual. Common foundations for achievement include the basic necessities of life such as food, water, and shelter, as well as other factors such as access to information and the skill and confidence to make sense of this. Foundations for achievement that are unique to the individual vary considerably however. Thus those that will help the elderly woman living alone to maximize her personal potential may be very different from those needed by the young gay man who at the age of 18 has been made to leave home by his parents.

Like the other four definitions we have considered, this one too has its weaknesses. It provides little guidance about the range of factors that might count as foundations for achievement. Neither is it entirely clear what personal potential is taken to be. Because of this, the notion of personal potential remains a little mystical, perhaps no more easily attainable than the 'state of complete mental, physical and social well being' that the World Health Organisation talked about in 1946.

## Lay beliefs about health

It should be clear by now that there is no one way of looking at health or health issues. Rather, there are a number of different perspectives that can be brought to bear on health matters. While the official perspective offered by modern bio-medicine currently holds sway in western society (see pp. 61–3), it co-exists alongside other official views, as well as lay beliefs about health issues. It is to these lay beliefs that we will now turn.

Research into lay beliefs about health has generally been anthropological in nature and has tried to examine the relationship between health beliefs and the broader cultural context in which they occur. Traditionally research of this kind took place in non-western societies, but more recently medical sociologists have begun to inquire into the lay beliefs of people living in Europe and North America.

## Being healthy

In contrast to modern bio-medical understandings which encourage us to see the body as a set of anatomical parts (the brain, the arms, the lungs, the heart, the liver) and physiological systems (the respiratory system, the digestive system, the skeletal system), many lay beliefs about health have their starting-point in the wholeness of human beings. Thus in Rory William's (1983) study of the health beliefs of elderly people living in Aberdeen, it was found that people could consider themselves, or others, healthy even though they may be badly diseased. What seemed to matter was the wholeness or the integrity of the person, their inner strength, and their ability to cope. So long as these remained intact, their healthiness remained.

An earlier study carried out in France by Claudine Herzlich (1973) came to similar conclusions, although she was able to distinguish a number of other ways of thinking about health in addition to those highlighted by Williams's research. From her analysis of in-depth interviews in Paris and Normandy, Herzlich was able to distinguish three different dimensions of health in the accounts she listened to. First, she identified a conception of health as a state of being – the absence of

13

illness. Second, she identified a view of health as something to be had – a reserve of physical strength, as well as the potential to resist illness. Finally, she identified an understanding of health as a state of doing – the full realization of an individual's reserve of health. This latter condition is rarely achieved but is characterized by happiness, relaxation, feeling strong, and getting on well with others.

Other research into lay beliefs about health suggests that some people may define health in functional terms – as the ability to carry out certain roles and responsibilities. Mildred Blaxter and Elizabeth Paterson (1982), for example, found this in their study of mothers' and daughters' health beliefs. Here they found that a popular way of understanding health was in terms of the ability to carry out normal daily routines.

It is important to recognize, however, that lay beliefs about health may vary according to the status and social background of the individual. Thus it is not implausible to suggest that the lay beliefs of middle-class people may differ systematically from those who are less advantaged. Similarly there may be gender and ethnic differences in lay beliefs about health. Systematic research into these differences has yet to be carried out, although there are a few studies which suggest that inquiry of this kind will be important.

With respect to social class, for example, Michael Calnan's (1987) recent work suggests that there are systematic differences between working-class and middle-class women's views on health. For middle-class women, health tends to be associated with 'being fit', 'being active', and 'taking exercise'. Middle-class women also made greater reference to health being something which enables people to cope with crises and stresses in life. For working-class women, on the other hand, health was more often equated with 'never being ill' and the ability to 'get through the day'. Curiously these class differences were very much less evident when respondents were asked to talk about their own health than when they were asked to talk about health in general.

*Being ill*

Cross-cultural research by anthropologists has identified a variety of lay beliefs about the causes of illness. Some societies explain the onset of illness by recourse to *supernatural forces*: wrathful gods or ancestral spirits who inflict suffering on those who have broken moral codes, or the forces conjured up by witches and sorcerers. Sometimes a personal quality is given to these forces which are said actively to seek out individuals who have incurred their wrath (Foster 1983). On other occasions, supernatural intervention may be felt to have been triggered by a general imbalance between a community of people and the environment within which they live. Sometimes illness is perceived as *retribution* for wrong-doing. On other occasions it may be seen as an honour or gift which allows the individual concerned to get closer to God.

Inquiry of this kind has also enabled social scientists to distinguish between lay beliefs which suggest that illness is caused by forces outside the individual (exogenous beliefs) and lay beliefs which imply that illness has its origins within the person concerned (endogenous beliefs). *Exogenous* lay beliefs often emphasize the role of external agents such as germs, 'bad air', contagion, the environment, stress, and debilitating work as factors responsible for illness. *Endogenous* beliefs, on the other hand, often emphasize inborn dispositions, heredity, and genetic defects as the causes of ill-health.

We can see these kinds of beliefs in the responses Mildred Blaxter (1983) obtained in her interviews with working-class women in Scotland. Infection by an outside agent was by far the most common explanation offered for the illnesses they experienced, but heredity, environmental hazards, stress, childbearing, trauma, and surgery were also identified as key factors that could result in the onset of ill health.

Similar ideas have also been found in a recent study by Ian Warwick, Peter Aggleton, and Hilary Homans (1988) of young people's beliefs about AIDS. In the course of their

15

in-depth interviews, they found a variety of exogenous and endogenous beliefs. Some respondents suggested for example that HIV infection might be acquired from the environment and from the people they mixed with. A few subscribed to the view that close proximity to an infected person might pose the risk of infection. Others were of the opinion that AIDS, like cancer, so these same respondents believed, could be found within each and every one of us. All that was needed was the right trigger to make it appear. Beliefs like these, which persist in spite of numerous health education campaigns, are not of course confined to young people. They are also shared by adults, some of whom may be professionally involved in health issues.

## Official definitions and lay beliefs

Amongst some health professionals there is a tendency to underplay the importance of lay beliefs about health. It may be implied that they are simply factual inaccuracies or wilful attempts to misconstrue modern bio-medical knowledge. Nothing could be further from the truth. Lay beliefs about health are the consequence of people's attempts to make sense of the various sources of information to which they have access. There is not one source of health information in the world in which we live. Rather, information about health matters comes from many different sources, and popular perceptions of health arise from the attempts people make to seek order where often there is often chaos and confusion. As such, lay beliefs about health are *syncretic* (Fitzpatrick 1984), drawing on a wide and disparate set of sources. They are also pragmatic, in that they enable us to cope with the complexity of health issues and to make apparent sense of our lives.

---

## Activities

Think for a moment about where your knowledge of the following things comes from. Does it come from your parents,

16

friends, magazines, television, the radio, the doctor, or from elsewhere? What have you learned from each source? Make a list of your main sources of information for each item on the list and the things you have learned from each. Do some of the things you have learned contradict one another? Compare your list with that of a friend.

- flu
- greasy hair
- athlete's foot
- spots
- chilblains
- smoking

The power of lay beliefs is shown dramatically in Cecil Helman's (1978) study of what he describes as 'medical folklore in a north London suburb'. The starting-point for his research was the often-heard saying 'Feed a cold, starve a fever', but his inquiries soon took him beyond this to consider some of the ways in which a wide range of illnesses were popularly understood. He noted, for example, that people attending the practice in which he worked (Helman was a general practitioner as well as a social scientist) distinguished between hot illnesses such as fevers, and cold illnesses such as chills or colds. It is important to recognize that people's feelings of abnormal temperature bore little relationship to bio-medical definitions of 'normal' body temperature (37°C).

From knowing which category an illness fell into, Helman found it possible to predict its perceived cause, its preferred treatment, and its likely outcome. For example, colds and chills were popularly understood as arising from the individual's relationship with the environment. Dampness, a cold wind or a draught, more often than not, were felt to have penetrated the person's head or feet, perhaps after they had had a hot bath or after they had washed their hair or had it cut. The appropriate treatment in such cases was a warm bed and plenty of hot drinks. Fevers, on the other hand, were popularly perceived as arising from 'germs' or 'bugs', malevolent entities transmitted through the air, via food or by close contact. Once within the body, these 'germs' moved around, 'finding their way to the chest', 'going to the head', or 'causing havoc in the bowels'. Appropriate treatment involved the administration of plenty of fluids in an attempt to 'flush out' the offending organism.

Helman's work is important in a number of respects. First, it identifies the complex relationship that exists between lay health beliefs and mainstream bio-medical knowledge. When judged against the latter, it would seem that lay beliefs are not entirely 'wrong'. For example, some fevers are indeed caused by viruses and bacteria, and the focus of infection can change throughout the course of a disease. Second, doctors and other health professionals may share some of the lay beliefs of their patients. It is perhaps in these terms that we can best make sense of the millions of gallons of cough mixture that are prescribed annually to help 'flush out' chest infections, and the continued prescribing by doctors of antibiotics for the many viral infections which are not amenable to control by drugs of this kind.

## Activities

In order to examine the relationship between professional explanations of health and lay health beliefs, carry out the following mini-research project.
1 Talk to six people you do not already know and ask them to think back to the last time they had a headache. What were the causes of the headache? What brought it on? Note down their replies.
2 Now ask them about each of the following things: a temperature, a cold, spots, the runs (diarrhoea), a cough. Add one or two extra items to this list if you like. Note down their replies.
3 With a friend, sort through your list of causes for each complaint. Allocate each cause to one of two categories,

depending on whether it is a bio-medical explanation (one that doctors are likely to approve of) or whether it reflects your respondent's lay beliefs about health.
4 Discuss where these lay beliefs came from. Are they ones that are widely shared?

## Measuring health

The majority of techniques used to measure health have their starting-point in the negative definitions of health discussed earlier (pp. 6–8). That is, instead of measuring health directly as the presence of certain qualities in the population, they measure it rather more obliquely in terms of the extent to which disease and illness are detected. Maybe this is a reflection of the debates about how best to define health in positive terms. Perhaps also it is an index of the extent to which we live in a world in which higher priority is given to the treatment of disease than to the promotion of health and well-being.

The study of disease in human populations is called *epidemiology*. Epidemiologists are usually interested in at least three things. The first of these is the distribution of disease within a particular group or population. Here they may wish to find out who is most affected, what their characteristics are and where they are located. Their second interest is in the causes of disease. By examining disease patterns, it is often possible to identify its causes. For example, John Snow's study of the 1854 cholera epidemic in London led him to notice that the disease was particularly prevalent in the area surrounding a particular water pump – the Broad Street water pump in Soho. This led him to suggest that the disease might be spread by contaminated water: a view which has since proved to be correct, but which at the time ran contrary to most medical opinion. Finally, epidemiologists may be interested in what happens after someone has a disease. Here they may find themselves plotting the course taken by particular diseases, the effectiveness of different kinds of therapies, and the likely outcome if treatment does not take place.

In carrying out their work, epidemiologists measure health in a variety of ways. Two of these measures are of particular importance. First, they may be interested in mortality – the ages at which people die and the causes of death. Second, they may be interested in morbidity, or sickness.

*Mortality*

For over a hundred years, numbers of deaths and age at death have been reliably recorded. From a knowledge of the number of deaths and the size of the population, it is possible to calculate what is known as the *crude death-rate*, the number of deaths per thousand population. In England and Wales in 1976 this was 12.1 per thousand. However, crude death-rates can be very misleading. As Donald Acheson and Spencer Hagard (1984) have put it,

> the crude death rate provides a very incomplete ... picture of the amount of serious disease in the population. For, other things being equal, the more old people there are in a population, the higher the crude death rate will be: the crude death rate is lower in Birmingham than Bournemouth and in Ebbw Vale than Llandudno, not because Birmingham and Ebbw Vale are healthier, but because Bournemouth and Llandudno are places to which many elderly people move after retirement.

(Acheson and Hagard 1984: 59)

Because of these difficulties, and because it may sometimes be important to identify death-rates within particular age groups, *age-specific death-rates* are often calculated by epidemiologists. Two age-specific death-rates are of special importance. These are the *stillbirth rate*, which tells us of every thousand births registered, how many were stillbirths, and the *infant mortality rate*, which is the number of deaths in infants under 1 year of age for every 1,000 live births registered. Yet another age-specific measure of mortality is *expectation of life* at birth, or the average length of life.

While we can be reasonably confident about the accuracy of statistics about the number of people who die each year and the age at which they die, we can be less certain about causes of death. The problem here is that doctors are asked to make a subjective judgement about the cause of death when filling in the death certificate. In some cases, this might be quite a straightforward thing to do. But fashions in diagnosis change and new diagnoses come into being. There is an additional issue to contend with in the case of those who have abnormalities in a number of their bodily systems. When they die there may be difficulty in identifying which of these problems was the principal cause of death. Nevertheless, death-rates from particular causes are sometimes calculated (sometimes on an age-specific basis), but care must be taken when interpreting them to remember the difficulties doctors often face when trying to determine the cause of death.

One of the greatest limitations of mortality statistics as a measure of health is that they provide a measure only of the kinds of ill-health that are fatal. They therefore provide little information about the kinds of disablement, pain, and suffering that do not lead to loss of life. Because of this, morbidity statistics are often collected.

## Morbidity

Morbidity or sickness can be measured in a variety of ways. Some of these measures focus on disease, whereas others are more concerned with illness (see pp. 6–8). This can create problems when comparisons are made between different sets of statistics. When examining morbidity statistics, it is important to be clear which of these two dimensions of health they focus on.

Valuable statistical data about morbidity can be obtained from hospital records, from consultations between patients and doctors, from records detailing the causes of absence from work, as well as from special surveys. Regardless of the kinds of data collected, epidemiologists take care to distinguish between the incidence of a disease or illness and its prevalence. By the term *incidence*, they mean the number of new cases occurring over a particular period of time. By the term *prevalence*, they mean the number of people who actually have the disease or illness at a particular moment. Knowing these numbers, plus the total number at risk, it is possible to calculate the incidence rate and the prevalence rate (usually per 10,000 or per 100,000 population) for a specific disease or illness.

A variety of data collection systems provide estimates of health by measuring the incidence and prevalence of disease. In the early 1950s the Hospital In-Patient Enquiry (HIPE) was established in England and Wales. This records the clinical characteristics of one in ten hospital in-patients. This source of data was supplemented in the 1970s by the Hospital Activity Analysis (HAA) completed by Regional Health Authorities. This details demographic and clinical data on all patients for every occasion on which they receive in-patient care. Both of these systems suffer from limitations in that they collect data on episodes of care rather than individual patients. Thus someone who returns to hospital several times will have the same effect on the statistics as several individuals admitted once. Information about those who consult general practitioners is available, if a little irregularly, from the General Practice Morbidity Survey conducted jointly by the Royal College of General Practitioners, the Office of Population Censuses and Surveys, and the Department of Health.

Both of these sources of information suffer from the fact that the information they record is likely to be influenced by a host of factors other than the true incidence of disease. The decision whether or not to seek help from a doctor, for example, may be as much affected by factors such as social class, domestic circumstances, and the local availability of services as by the presence or absence of disease itself.

Certificates of incapacity for work provide a less than adequate source of information on morbidity. For a start, most of the population are not employed, and in Britain a self-certificating system applies for the first few days of sickness, whereby individuals are free to write down in their own words the nature of their incapacity. On some occasions, their descriptions will identify a self-diagnosed disease, on others it will be the subjective feelings of illness that are described. With more than a week's absence from work, a doctor's certificate is required, but here too there may be reasons to question the validity of the information given. As Acheson and Hagard put it,

> the reason given on the medical certificate for sickness absence is imprecise and sometimes unreliable or even misleading, for the general practitioner knows that his [sic] certificate will be seen by the patient and by a number of lay persons, including possibly the patient's employer. Hence the diagnosis he [sic] enters is often intentionally indeterminate.
>
> (Acheson and Hagard 1984: 64)

Specially commissioned surveys can also provide information about patterns of morbidity. Until recently, the *General Household Survey* (e.g. OPCS 1986) offered a valuable source of information about self-assessed sickness; a host of local surveys carried out each year provide more limited data like these.

It will be clear that major problems surround the collection and interpretation of health statistics. Most of the measures currently used focus not on health itself but on its absence. They aim to provide an estimate of health by identifying the extent to which death, disease, and illness are present in a given population. In interpreting health statistics, therefore, it is important to be aware of the shortcomings and limitations of different data collection procedures. Some of these are of a technical kind and relate to the manner in which statistics are collected. Others however are more wide-ranging, and relate to the principles and assumptions that underpin the procedures employed.

===

Activities

In this chapter you have been introduced to some of the key ideas that you will need throughout the rest of the book.
1 Without looking back, make some notes on the following topics: disease, illness, negative definitions of health, positive definitions of health, crude mortality rate, age-specific mortality rate, infant mortality rate, measures of morbidity, incidence, prevalence.
2 Now, check to make sure that the points you have made match those you have read about.

===

*Further reading*

*If you are interested in following up some of the debates about the nature of health you will find chapter 4 of Seedhouse's (1986) book particularly useful. Chapter 2 in Fitzpatrick et al. (1984) contains a useful summary of research into lay beliefs about illness, and there are a number of chapters in Currer and Stacey (1986) which detail findings from original inquiry in this field. A readable summary of Helman's work can be found in Part 1 of Black et al. (1984) and a more extended discussion of issues arising from attempts to measure health can be found in Chapter 5 in Book 1 (Studying Health and Disease) of the Open University (1985a) course Health and Disease (U205). Finally, chapters 5 and 6 of Cornwell (1984) provide a graphic insight into the experience of health and illness in a group of households in the East End of London.*

# 2

# *Measuring health*

In a recent book, Jeanette Mitchell (1984) examines a range of popular misconceptions about ill-health. One of these is the myth that ill-health usually strikes at random, or as she puts it 'without apparent rhyme or reason'. In order to evaluate this claim, she looks at some of the data from Geoffrey Rose and Michael Marmot's (1981) study of mortality amongst a cohort of 17,000 male civil servants working in Whitehall, London. In the first seven years of the research, over a thousand civil servants died, almost half of them from heart attacks. However, when the data are examined more closely it seems that the lower the grade, the higher the mortality. For example, men in the lowest grades (messengers and those doing unskilled work) had a death-rate almost four times as large as the top civil servants. Similarly men in the clerical grades had a death-rate three times greater than those in the top grades, and men in the professional and executive grades had a death-rate twice that of their more senior colleagues. Clearly amongst people like these at least there is a clear pattern when it comes to mortality.

Rose and Marmot's work was carried out amongst men, and the health differences they detect relate primarily to the occupational background, or class, of the individuals concerned. Similar studies have been carried out amongst women for a variety of other health measures. For example, data are available from the 1984 *General Household Survey* (OPCS 1986) to suggest that there are class differences among women in the extent to which they experienced serious long-standing illness, with 9 per cent of women in social class I (professional) reporting this compared with 34 per cent in social class V (unskilled). This same report showed that whereas women in social class 1 reported an average of eighteen days' restricted activity per year, their counterparts in social class V reported an average of forty-three days (OPCS 1986). There are, however, problems in analysing data like these since, in the majority of studies, married women are allocated the social class of their husband. Frequently this fails to do justice to the real conditions under which many women live: particularly when material factors to do with the home, with child-care, and with paid employment outside the home all need to be taken into account.

There is also evidence to suggest that ill-health is far from evenly distributed in Britain on the grounds of ethnicity. While there are major problems with the statistical evidence here too, in that the ethnic origins of individuals have to be inferred from their place of birth, available evidence tends to suggest that in England and Wales at least there is strikingly high mortality from strokes and to a lesser extent other circulatory disease, amongst both women and men born in the African and Caribbean Commonwealth (Marmot *et al.* 1984).

Nevertheless, from these and other studies, it is clear that ill-health is *not* randomly distributed across the population. Some groups are more likely to be healthy than others, regardless of the measure chosen, whereas others are more likely to experience illness or disease. In this chapter we shall examine some of the key inequalities in health that currently exist. The main focus will be on British experience, although reference will be made to relevant international data where appropriate. The emphasis will be on description rather than explanation. In Chapters 3–6 we shall look at some of the different ways in which these patterns can be explained.

## Some words of caution

Before we proceed, some words of caution. It is tempting to assume when looking at health statistics that the facts will somehow speak for themselves, especially when they appear in the form of tables and graphs. Unfortunately this is far from true. Already in this chapter we have seen how assumptions are made when particular kinds of health statistics are collected. For example, some sociologists feel it is appropriate to equate social class with occupation. Others feel it justifiable to allocate married women to the social class of their spouse. Yet others feel it is sufficient to identify racial and ethnic differences on the basis of country of birth. While assumptions like these make data collection easier, they impose limits on the kinds of conclusions that can legitimately be reached when findings are subsequently analysed. It is vitally important therefore to be aware of the limitations of the categories used to classify data in health research.

It is also important to remember that theory is not just something that emerges from data, it also affects the kinds of data collected, the way in which they are presented, and the kind of analysis that is carried out. Thus social researchers can *choose* to examine the relationship between any one measure of health and a host of other variables such as age, class, sex, and race. Which of these variables they select depends on the kind of theory they want to construct.

The variable most examined in research into health inequalities is that of class. Indeed some books make little reference to dimensions other than this. Here, however, the emphasis will be on a range of health inequalities including those to do with sex, age, and ethnicity. While our concern

Figure 2  Selected causes of death by age and sex, England, Wales, Scotland, and Northern Ireland, 1979

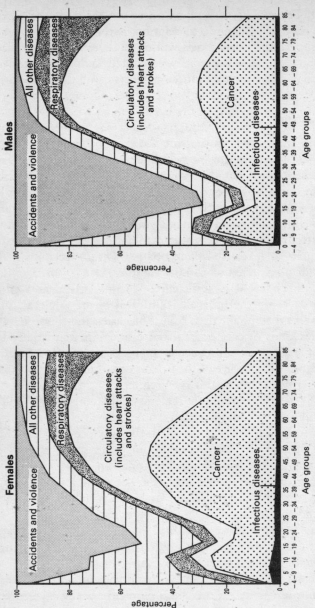

Source: What is to be Done about Illness and Health? by Jeanette Mitchell (Penguin Books, 1984), copyright © The Socialist Society, 1984, pp. 28–9. Reproduced by permission of Penguin Books Ltd.

will be with two variables – a measure of health and another variable which accounts for variations in this – it is important to recognize that in the real world, most health inequalities are best accounted for not by one variable but by a number of factors. Class, age, sex, and ethnicity, as well as related influences such as housing and employment, all interact to affect life chances. For example, the health threats to a 48-year-old Bengali working in the clothing industry may be very different from those facing a 34-year-old Greek-Cypriot workng in a bank. Some of these differences may be due to the age, others to sex and ethnicity, yet others to class. Similarly the health problems confronting a 21-year-old polytechnic student with no dependants may be very different from those facing an unemployed person of similar age with child-care responsibility.

Figure 2 shows how two variables (sex and age) interact to affect mortality. If further graphs were drawn to show mortality for women and men of different social classes, the interaction between three (sex, age, and class) rather than two variables affecting health could be studied.

---

Activities

In order to check that you understand the data in Figure 2, answer the following questions and compare your responses with those of your friends and tutor.

1 For men overall, what were the two most likely causes of death in 1979?
2 For women overall, what were the two most likely causes of death in 1979?
3 In 1979, what was the most likely cause of death for a woman aged between 35 and 39? What was the most likely cause of death for a man of the same age?
4 In 1979, what was the most likely cause of death for a man aged between 50 and 54? What was the most likely cause of death for a woman of the same age?

---

Figure 3  *Age-specific mortality rates of males, Egypt (1976) and England and Wales (1979)*

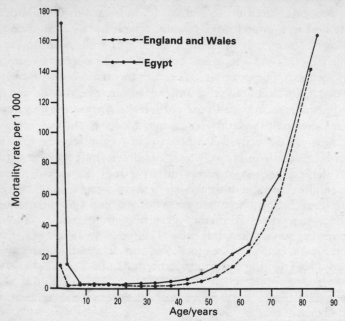

*Source*: United Nations (1981). Reproduced in Open University (1985c) p. 9

## Age and health inequalities

### *Mortality*

Earlier, a distinction was made between the crude death-rate and age-specific death-rates (p. 20). Because crude death-rates tend to mask age differences in mortality, they are rarely calculated when sensitive measures of health are needed. Instead a range of age-specific death-rates will be worked out. Alternatively one key age-specific death-rate, usually the infant mortality rate, will be examined.

If a series of age-specific death-rates is calculated, it is possible to represent them diagrammatically as in Figure 3. This particular diagram compares the age-specific mortality

Table 1    *Selected infant mortality rates (per 1,000 live births)*

| Country | Rate |
| --- | --- |
| Japan | 7 |
| Sweden | 7 |
| USA | 12 |
| Jamaica | 16 |
| USSR | 28 |
| China | 49 |
| Brazil | 82 |
| Egypt | 110 |
| India | 122 |
| Bangladesh | 140 |
| Sierra Leone | 215 |

*Source*: United Nations (1981)

rates of men in England and Wales with those in Egypt. A graph like this offers an indication of the points in the life-cycle at which mortality is likely to be highest. It does this fairly crudely because the data in the graph have been collected *cross-sectionally* – that is at one moment in time. While a diagram like this tells us something about the mortality of different age groups today, it reveals little about the mortality of these same age groups in the past.

Activities

1 Look at the data in Figure 3. What major differences can you detect between the age-specific mortality curve for England and Wales and that for Egypt?
2 How might these differences be accounted for?
Discuss your conclusions with others in small groups. How would you check out whether or not your explanations are correct?

Infant mortality rates record the number of deaths in the first year of life per 1,000 live births. In countries where reliable records of births and deaths are kept, infant mortality can be calculated with some precision. Infant mortality rates are often used as indicators of socio-economic development – as measures of general standards of health and welfare provision (see Table 1).

## Activities

1 Look at the data in Table 1 and make a list of the factors you think might account for the differences in infant mortality rates between countries such as Bangladesh and Sierra Leone and countries such as the USA.
2 Now make a list of the factors that might account for the regional differences in infant mortality recorded in Table 2.
3 Discuss your lists with others in small groups. What factors are common to both lists? What factors are specific to a particular list?

Care needs to be taken, however, in interpreting infant mortality rates since the global figure for a particular country can conceal important regional and ethnic variations. For example, in South Africa there is a large difference between the infant mortality rate of Blacks and Whites, and in England there is variation from one health region to another (see Table 2).

*Morbidity*

In Europe and North America, age variations in morbidity tend to follow a similar pattern to age differences in mortality – that is, the older people are, the more ill-health they are likely to experience. As an illustration of this, Figure 4 plots

Table 2    *Selected regional variations in infant mortality, England, 1987*

| Region | Rate |
| --- | --- |
| East Anglia | 7.8 |
| NW Thames | 8.3 |
| Northern | 8.7 |
| Trent | 9.1 |
| Wessex | 9.5 |
| Yorkshire | 10.1 |

*Source*: House of Commons (1988)

Figure 4    *Incidence of selected cancers in males by age, England and Wales, 1970*

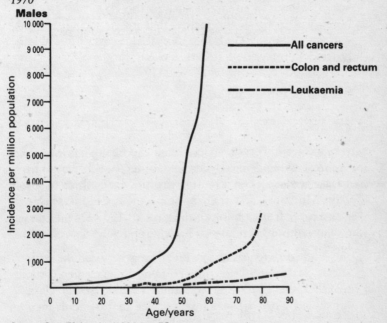

*Source*: Open University (1985c) p. 76

the incidence of three types of cancer against age for men in England and Wales.

33

It is important to realize, however, that in Europe and North America it is not until people are in their early 70s that they are likely to be significantly affected by chronic limiting illness. As Fennell *et al.* (1988: 110) have recently pointed out, 'growing old is far from necessarily accompanied by becoming sick, (after all) by definition, older people are the "survivors"'.

Recent research suggests that there are important sex differences between women and men in the kind of illness that is reported with increasing old age. In Britain, women in the older age groups are more likely than men to report long-standing or disabling illness (Victor 1987). Furthermore, whereas women are more likely to report mobility problems and visual impairment in old age, men are more likely to report hearing difficulties (Hunt 1978). Care should be taken in interpreting these data, however, since class differences also have a role to play in determining patterns of morbidity.

## Class and health inequalities

*Mortality*

The relationship between social class and health has long been of interest to epidemiologists and other health researchers, not least because it can identify priorities for health and social policy. Moreover, it would appear that class differences in health are far from a thing of the past. In 1977 David Ennals, the then Labour Secretary of State for Social Services, said:

the crude differences in mortality rates between the various social classes are worrying. To take the extreme example, in 1971 the death-rate for adult men in social class V (unskilled workers) was nearly twice that of adult men in social class I (professional workers) ... when you look at death-rates for specific diseases the gap is even wider ... the first step towards remedial action is to put together what is already known about the problem ... it is a major challenge for the next ten or more years to try to narrow the gap in health standards between different social classes.

(quoted in Townsend and Davidson 1982: 14)

Following this statement, a Research Working Group chaired by Sir Douglas Black, formerly Chief Scientist at the Department of Health and at the time President of the Royal College of Physicians, was set up to examine inequalities in health and make relevant policy recommendations. The Research Working Group considered a variety of measures of class in going about its work. In the end though, it settled for the Registrar General's classification. This allocates individuals to one of six groups on the basis of occupation – Professional (Social Class I), Managerial and Lower Professional (Social Class II), Skilled Non-manual (Social Class IIIN), Skilled Manual (IIIM), Partly Skilled (IV), and Unskilled (V). While there are clear problems with this system of classification, not least because it has difficulty accommodating the distinctive experience of women, unemployed people, young people living away from home, retired persons and so on, a wide range of health statistics are collected annually using it. This allows for some degree of comparability over time.

The Research Working Group submitted its report in early 1980. Its principal findings pointed to the continued existence of profound inequalities in mortality at birth, in childhood, and in adulthood. In order to compare different mortality across different occupational groups, a statistic called the *Standardised Mortality Ratio* (SMR) was calculated for each class. For any particular age group, this provides a measure of the extent to which the mortality rate of each social class differs from the average of the age group as a whole. If a class has an SMR of 100, then its mortality rate is the same as that for the age group as a whole. If a class has an SMR less than 100, then its mortality rate is less than that of the age group as a whole, and if it has an SMR greater than 100, then its mortality rate is greater than that for the age group as a whole. Figure 5 presents some of the main findings from the

35

Figure 5  *Mortality by occupational class and age, 1970–2*

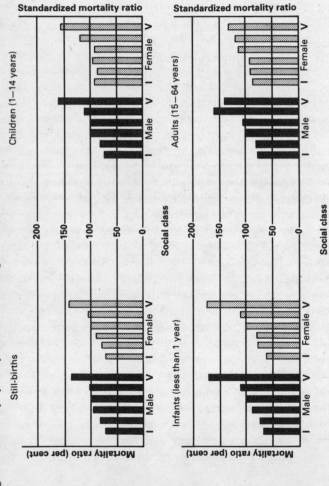

*Source:* OPCS (1978), Occupational Mortality 1970–2, series DS no. 1 (HMSO)

*Black Report* (in Townsend and Davidson 1982), as the study came to be known.

The implications of class differences such as these cannot be over-estimated. As Peter Townsend and Nick Davidson put it in their introduction to the *Report*:

> If the mortality rates of occupational class I (professional workers and members of their families) had applied to classes IV and V (partly skilled and unskilled manual workers and their families) during 1970–2, 74,000 lives of people under 75 would not have been lost. This estimate included nearly 10,000 children and 32,000 men aged 15 to 64 . . . . During the twenty years up to the early 1970s . . . the mortality rates for both men and women aged 35 and over in occupational classes I and II steadily diminished, while those in IV and V changed very little or even deteriorated.
>
> (Townsend and Davidson 1982: 15)

In 1986, less than ten years later, an update on the *Black Report* was commissioned by the then Health Education Council (now the Health Education Authority), and in early 1987 *The Health Divide* (Townsend *et al.* 1988) was published. The distinct class gradients in stillbirths, infant mortality, and adult mortality were still present (Figure 6), and while the author of the report, Margaret Whitehead, acknowledged the difficulties in measuring health trends over time, she concluded on the basis of the many studies reviewed that there was

> convincing evidence of a widening of health inequalities between social groups in recent decades, especially in adults. Indeed, in some respects the health of the lower occupational classes has actually been deteriorating against the background of a general improvement in the population as a whole.
>
> (Townsend *et al.* 1988: 266)

37

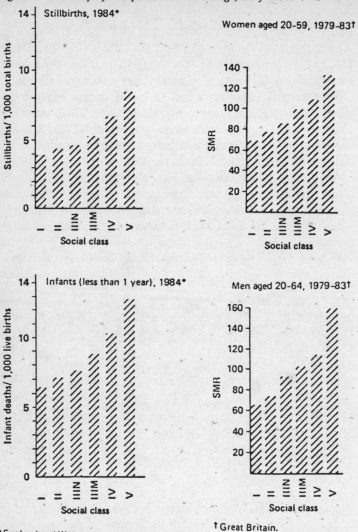

Figure 6  *Mortality by occupational class and age, early 1980s*

*England and Wales.

† Great Britain.

*Sources*: OPCS (1983 and 1984) Mortality statistics, perinatal and infant: social and biological factors 1984, series DH3, no. 17 (HMSO), and OPCS Occupational mortality, decennial supplement 1979–83, series DS, no. 6 (HMSO)

Lest it be thought that class differences are restricted only to mortality, there is evidence in both the *Black Report* and *The Health Divide* to suggest that occupational groups differ from one another in the extent to which they experience illness.

Much of the data reviewed in both reports come from national studies of the prevalence of disease in different social groups. For example, there have been national sample surveys of the prevalence of diseases such as bronchitis. As part of these, selected GPs have been asked to collect information on the occupational backgrounds of the individuals affected. Other data which shed light on class differences in morbidity come from GPs' consultation records, although given that a doctor's main interest during a consultation is unlikely to be the patient's social class, there are problems with the reliability of these kinds of data! Finally, the *General Household Survey* (e.g. OPCS 1986) collects data on acute and chronic illness.

When these various sources of information are put together, various patterns emerge. Throughout the 1980s, for example, a clear class gradient can be found in most measures of morbidity. The gradient is steepest for serious long-standing illness, where the rate amongst unskilled manual workers (both women and men) is more than double that for professionals. There are also marked class differences in the prevalence of less serious long-standing illness. For acute sickness on the other hand, the differential becomes evident only after the age of 45 (Townsend *et al.* 1988). More recent research into morbidity as part of the Health and Life-Style Survey also reveals consistent class differences in a variety of self-reported measures of morbidity (Blaxter 1987).

There is also some evidence that class differences in morbidity may be getting wider. After analysing trends in acute and chronic illness recorded by the *General Household Survey* between 1974 and 1984, Margaret Whitehead concludes:

Manual groups had higher rates of long-term illness than non-manual groups throughout the decade and the gap between the two groups widened over the ten year period. For men, the widening occurred particularly from 1974 to 1979 and since then the gap has remained fairly stable. For women, the gap between manual and non-manual groups widened throughout the 1970s and continued to widen the 1980s. In both men and women, rates of acute illness were consistently higher for manual than for non-manual groups. There was a slight widening of the gap between the two groups between 1974 and 1979, and then it remained stable up to 1984.

(Townsend *et al.* 1988: 262–3)

Table 3  *Annual death-rates per 1,000 people within each age group, England and Wales, 1982*

| Age | Women | Men |
|---|---|---|
| 1–4 | 9.5 | 12.3 |
| 5–14 | 0.4 | 0.5 |
| 15–24 | 0.3 | 0.8 |
| 25–34 | 0.5 | 0.9 |
| 35–44 | 1.2 | 1.8 |
| 45–54 | 3.6 | 5.9 |
| 55–64 | 9.7 | 17.5 |
| 65–74 | 24.3 | 45.8 |
| 75–84 | 65.8 | 105.5 |
| 85+ | 178.2 | 223.2 |

*Source*: OPCS (1982) Table 3

## Sex and health inequalities

*Mortality*

In 1988 it was estimated that on average new-born girls could expect to live six years longer than new-born boys, to 78 and 72 years respectively (Central Office of Information 1989).

Furthermore, as the data in Table 3 show, the death-rate for men clearly exceeds that for women in every age group. In Britain the gap in life expectancy between women and men has steadily increased over the last forty years.

There are significant differences between women and men when it comes to cause of death. Figure 2 on p. 28 identifies the major causes of death for women and men of different ages. About 40 per cent of the difference in overall mortality between the sexes can be accounted for by men's greater susceptibility to heart disease. Mortality from cancer is also higher in men than it is in women, although it is important to recognize that women and men differ in their vulnerability to different kinds of cancers.

## Morbidity

While on average men tend to die earlier than women, women experience more sickness than men. They are more likely to report chronic and acute illness and to consult their doctor about this. However, gross trends such as these conceal a number of important variations. For example, the recent National Survey of Health and Development found that amongst 21–25-year-olds, serious illness was more common in young men than in young women (Wadsworth 1986). It was also recently reported that in 1983, boys between 5 and 15 were more likely to report a long-standing illness than girls, a pattern which was reversed for the over-65s (OPCS 1985). Moreover, if a woman's employment status is taken into consideration, it would seem that among women with children, paid employment is associated with less illness for middle-class women, but more illness for working-class women. Clearly there are some complex interactions here between sex, age, and employment status.

Sex differences in mortality and morbidity raise some interesting questions about why, if men consistently out-number women in the risk of premature death, they experience less illness or seek medical help less often. At the present time we do not know why this is the case, but a variety of factors may affect women and men differently in this respect. For example, higher GP consultation rates amongst women may be partially accountable for in terms of the greater stresses they may face in maintaining the multiple roles of housewife, mother, and employee. Moreover, social pressures may encourage men to neglect their physical health and be selective in their use of medical services.

## Culture, ethnicity, and health inequalities

### Mortality

In studying cultural and ethnic inequalities in health, a major difficulty arises when it comes to defining and operationalizing the concept of race. Much recent writing uses terms such as 'ethnic minorities' and 'minority ethnic groups' to identify those who share a common cultural heritage and who experience varying degrees of discrimination (Donovan 1984). It is vitally important, however, to recognize that while all minority ethnic groups may experience discrimination and disadvantage, the form and intensity that this takes varies significantly from one group to another. Care should therefore be taken to guard against the tendency to assume that the health problems facing different minority ethnic groups are the same.

Even though Britain is a multicultural society, few health surveys have systematically collected data on ethnic inequalities in health. It was not until 1984, for example, that the first comprehensive study of mortality amongst ethnic minorities was carried out in England and Wales. Before then, a variety of small-scale local studies had to be relied on to identify the health problems experienced by such groups in Britain. Sadly, in the majority of these studies, researchers have relied on the country of birth recorded on birth and death certificates in order to infer the ethnic backgrounds of the individuals concerned. This means that health data on the British-born children of ethnic minorities tend to be lacking. Indeed, apart from infant mortality data, there is still very little information about the health of British-born children of ethnic minorities.

From the data available, it would seem that most health problems experienced by members of minority ethnic groups are similar in kind, but different in intensity, to those already present within the wider community. The first study of *Immigrant Mortality in England and Wales* (Marmot *et al.* 1984) did, however, identify above-average SMRs for women and men born in the African Commonwealth, and women born in the Indian subcontinent and the Caribbean Commonwealth. Additionally all the minority groups surveyed had higher than average mortality for tuberculosis and accidents, but lower than average mortality for diseases such as bronchitis. Amongst those from the Caribbean and the African Commonwealth, there was strikingly high mortality from hypertension and high mortality from strokes compared in comparison with the national averages for England and Wales.

Figure 7 contrasts infant mortality in England and Wales for mothers born in Pakistan, India, Bangladesh, and the Caribbean compared with those born elsewhere. For mothers from ethnic minority groups, infant mortality would seem to be consistently higher, but more variable, over the period concerned.

## Morbidity

Recent studies of morbidity suggest that certain diseases may be more prevalent amongst some minority ethnic groups than others. These include sickle cell disease amongst Afro-Caribbeans, and rickets and osteomalacia amongst those of Asian origin. Unusually high rates of hypertension (high blood pressure) have also been recorded amongst some people of Afro-Caribbean origin, as have high rates of tuberculosis among Asians.

Sickle cell disease is a general term used to describe a variety of genetically transmitted conditions in which red

43

Figure 7   *Infant mortality by maternal country of birth, England and Wales, 1975–84*

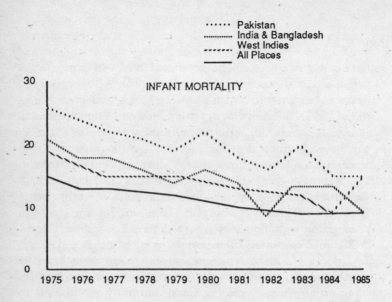

Source: Bhat *et al.* (1988) p. 182

blood cells function less efficiently than otherwise. As a result, the individual's health suffers, and they may experience pain, fatigue, and general debility, particularly in times of stress. It is estimated that about 1 in 400 people of Afro-Caribbean origin in Britain are affected by sickle cell disease, which is also widespread in parts of the Mediterranean and Africa (Grimsley and Bhat 1988).

Rickets, and its adult equivalent osteomalacia, is a disease which affects the developing skeleton, causing pain and swelling in the bones. Both of these conditions are caused by Vitamin D deficiency, and both were found to be prevalent in the 1970s amongst Asians living in Glasgow and Bradford (Goel 1976; Ford 1976).

## Regional inequalities in health

### Mortality

In the last ten years, considerable interest has been expressed in regional variations in health, and the *Black Report* was influential in drawing attention to regional variations in mortality rates. Using these as an indicator of health, the healthiest part of Britain would seem to be southern England, in particular the area south of a line drawn across the country from the Bristol Channel to the Wash (Townsend and Davidson 1982). It should be recognized, however, that this pattern is a relatively recent one. In the nineteenth century south-east England had a high death-rate, and Wales and the north were healthier parts of the country in which to live.

In *The Health Divide*, Margaret Whitehead offers a more refined analysis of some of the evidence presented in the *Black Report*. Mortality rates increase steadily as you move from the south and south-east to the north and north-west of the country. However, there is an important interaction between class and regional inequalities in health, with the gap between social class V and social class I being greatest in the north.

### Morbidity

Since the publication of the *Black Report*, data identifying regional differences in morbidity have become more widely available. This suggests that the north/south divide is present for most diseases. Arthritis, rheumatism, heart disease, bonchitis, and stomach disease all show this trend, as does depression (Cox 1987).

However, at the same time as these additional data have become available, researchers have grown more cautious when making generalizations about regional variations in health. It has been discovered, for example, that health differences often exist within the same administrative region. Thus there are relatively healthy and relatively unhealthy communities in the north, as there are within the south. Moreover, the healthiest areas in the north compare well with the healthiest areas in the south. This unevenness in the regional distribution of health was not initially detected by studies which considered regions only as a whole. This is not to say of course that the north/south health divide does not exist, it plainly does, but it is to qualify some of the cruder generalizations about this divide that have been made.

## International inequalities in health

The emphasis so far in this chapter has been on examining health inequalities in Britain. Clearly it would be inappropriate to conclude without considering the broader international context. It is vital to recognize, however, that significant age, class, sex, regional, and ethnic differences exist within the mortality and morbidity data to be described. A comprehensive study of these variations is beyond the scope of this book, although guidance is offered on appropriate sources of reference at the end of this chapter.

### Mortality

Reference was made earlier to international differences in age-specific mortality and infant mortality rates (pp. 30–2). The former provide an indication of critical points in the life-cycle when individuals are likely to experience health problems. The latter offer an indication of the overall socio-economic development of a country. Other measures of mortality which allow comparisons to be made between countries include the expectation of life at birth (see Table 4).

In making sense of international data on mortality, it is important to be sensitive not only to sex differences such as those identified in Table 4, but also to regional variations. In

Table 4  *Expectation of life at birth for selected countries*

| Country | Men | Women |
|---|---|---|
| Malawi | 41 | 44 |
| Sierra Leone | 44 | 48 |
| Bangladesh | 46 | 47 |
| Egypt | 52 | 54 |
| Brazil | 58 | 61 |
| Jamaica | 63 | 67 |
| USSR | 64 | 74 |
| China | 66 | 69 |
| England and Wales | 70 | 76 |
| USA | 70 | 78 |
| Sweden | 72 | 78 |
| Japan | 73 | 79 |

*Source*: United Nations (1981)

the case of many countries, the rural/urban divide may be significant, and care is needed in interpreting differences across this divide. Thus the infant mortality rate in rural Malawi has recently been reported as 135.1 per thousand live births, as against 71.0 in urban areas. Comparable figures from El Salvador, on the other hand, put infant mortality at 38.4 per thousand live births in rural areas, and 47.0 per thousand live births in urban areas (United Nations 1981). Without additional data by which to relate these figures to the standard of living and the quality of health care in rural and urban areas within the two countries, statistics like these are difficult to interpret.

## Morbidity

Similar difficulties can arise when examining international differences in morbidity. For a start, the population structures of countries may differ, which may in turn have consequences for patterns of disease. In some Third World countries, for example, up to half the population may be younger than 16.

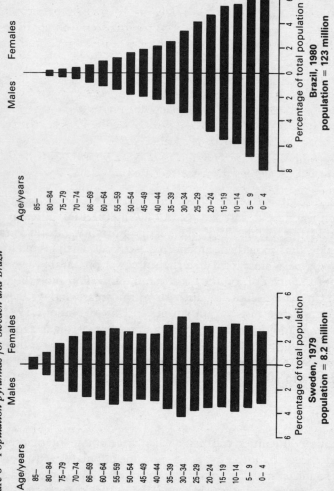

Figure 8  *Population pyramids for Sweden and Brazil*

Source: Open University (1985c)

In this kind of situation, infectious and parasitic diseases may be particularly prevalent. In developed countries, on the other hand, there may be a large ageing population, in which case chronic disease may be more of a problem.

The interaction between malnutrition, existing disease, and new infection can also give rise to specific patterns of morbidity which make clear-cut international comparisons difficult. For example, measles rarely causes death amongst children in Europe and North America, but in parts of the Third World its effects can be particularly serious since it can easily kill those already weakened by malnourishment or existing infections. Under these circumstances, to compare the consequences of the same disease in two different environments is not to compare like with like.

Another reason for caution in making international health comparisons comes from the fact that patterns of morbidity are constantly shifting. Partly this is in response to medical intervention, but partly it is as a consequence of more wide-ranging social change. As urbanization takes place in less developed countries, it is likely to affect existing patterns of disease but it brings with it new complaints.

Above all, it is the *interaction* between variables such as age, sex, occupation, region, locality, nutrition, and past patterns of infection that determines national and regional patterns of mortality and morbidity, and it is this interaction which needs to be taken into account when making sense of international health data.

Activities

Figure 8 consists of two population pyramids showing the relative numbers of women and men of different ages in the population. The first is from a European country (Sweden 1979), the second is from a Third World country (Brazil 1980).

1 Working with a partner, make a list of the health problems that you might expect to find in each country.

2 Rank these in terms of their overall prevalence, bearing in mind the number of people who are likely to be affected by each problem.
3 Discuss in small groups the implications of these differences for the kinds of health care that may need to be provided in each country.

*Further reading*

*If you want to find out more about health inequalities in Britain, there can be no substitute for reading the* Black Report *and* The Health Divide. *Both are available together in Townsend et al. (1988). The* United Nations Demographic Yearbook *(published annually and available in reference libraries) contains a wealth of international data on health inequalities. Chapter 5 of Book 1 (Studying Health and Disease) in the Open University's course* Health and Disease (U205) *describes some of the basic principles that underpin the analysis of the data presented in this chapter. Chapters 2, 3 and 9 of Book 3 (The Health of Nations) in the same course describes a number of international variations in patterns of mortality and morbidity. Chapter 7 in Bhat et al. (1988) offers a useful summary of racial and ethnic inequalities in health in Britain, whereas Graham (1985) contains an interesting discussion of sex inequalities in health.*

# 3

## *Explaining health*

For thousands of years, women and men have attempted to explain health and well-being, sickness and disease, life and death. The explanations they have come up with vary considerably according to the circumstances in which they were developed. Often these theories relate to broader beliefs about the make-up of the universe, the nature of human life, issues of predestination and of immortality, and questions of religion and God. Some of them may be more global than other, accounting for a wide range of health issues. Others may be more focused, offering an in-depth analysis of a more restricted range of problems. What all of them try to do is to order and make sense of the variety of health-related experiences people have, and to identify potentially useful health-care interventions.

The emphasis so far has been on describing rather than explaining patterns of health. In doing this, however, we have had to acknowledge that there can be no such thing as pure description. The categories we use to collect data have themselves been influenced by theory – 'theory' which tells researchers what kind of information it is important to collect when it comes to explaining health inequalities. Hence some social researchers collect data on the occupational background of those they talk with, others note down the sex of respondents, yet others identify the age or the ethnic origins of those whose lives they are studying. They do this because existing theory, or their own taken-for-granted assumptions, tell them that class, sex, age, and ethnicity may be important determinants of health.

On the other hand, when studying health inequalities, most social researchers nowadays do *not* collect data on variables such as the colour of the tongue, the length of a person's toenails, curses that may have been made, or spells that may have been cast. Still less are they interested in the flight patterns of birds, the phases of the moon, or the condition of sheep's entrails. This is because the modern theories which guide their data collection tell them that these variables are unlikely to be significant factors when it comes to explaining health. Thus data collection is heavily influenced by kinds of explanations that researchers feel it important to construct.

However, theories about the causes of health, disease, and illness vary widely from society to society. They also change over time. As a result, we live in a world in which there are *competing explanations* of health issues: some of which may be widely shared, some of which may be legacies from the past, and a few of which may be the forerunners of better theories to come. While at any one moment certain explanations may appear more sensible, more 'truth-like', than others, they must nevertheless be subjected to critical evaluation before decisions can be made about how adequate they really are.

In this chapter, an overview of different kinds of explanations will be offered (see Table 5). This distinguishes between a number of traditional ways of explaining health, disease, and illness and several more modern accounts. Three of these more modern kinds of explanations – social positivism, interactionism, and structuralism – will be examined in more detail later.

Table 5   *Competing explanations of health, disease, and illness*

| Traditional (main features developed before 1800) | Modern (main features developed after 1800) |
|---|---|
| Ayurvedic explanations | Bio-medical positivist explanations |
| Chinese explanations | Social-positivist explanations |
| Early European explanations | Interactionist explanations |
| | Structuralist explanations |

## Traditional explanations of health, disease, and illness

Traditional ideas about health, disease, and illness can be grouped into a number of relatively distinct perspectives. Three of these will be focused on here – those offered by Ayurvedic medicine, by Chinese medicine, and by European medicine up until the end of the eighteenth century. In the space available, it will not be possible to offer a comprehensive review of each account. Instead, the main features of each will be identified to provide a context against which to assess more modern theories.

Most traditional explanations differ significantly from more recent ones in that they emphasize the fundamental and irreducible wholeness of human beings – their *holism*. In contrast, by distinguishing between the mind and the body, and between anatomical parts (the heart, the brain, the liver, etc.) and physiological systems (the respiratory system, the nervous system, the digestive system, etc.) modern bio-medicine encourages us to view people in a more fragmented way. Traditional explanations also tend to emphasize the importance of *balance*, both within the person, and between people and their environments.

## Ayurvedic explanations

As far back as 600 BC, there were established centres of learning in India devoted to teaching about health and disease. Those who taught in them knew much about the different kinds of tissues that comprise the body as well as about digestive and reproductive processes. Indeed, it has been reported that as early as 500 BC Hindu medical schools were teaching birth control based on the rhythm method (Durant and Durant 1952).

Informing the practices of those who worked within these establishments were writings of a status not unlike that of today's medical textbooks. These writings recorded what was commonly understood to be true about people and the causes of ill-health. Some of them, such as the *Rg-Veda*, dated back as far as the second millenium BC. Others were of more recent origin. Writings in the *Rg-Veda* itself were regarded as the highest truth, the word *Veda* meaning wisdom or science, and Ayurvedic health practices are those that have their origin in this body of knowledge. They have been widely practised throughout the Indian subcontinent for thousands of years and are still practised there today. In Europe and North America they sometimes inform the actions of those who work in what is sometimes called complementary medicine, complementary that is to modern bio-medicine.

According to Ayurvedic thought, health results when there is balance between three primary humours: wind (vayu), gall (pitta), and mucus (kapha). This balance is usually achieved when there is equilibrium between the person as a whole and his or her environment. When this stability is disturbed, one or more of the primary humours becomes out of balance with the others and ill-health results. This in turn may have consequences for one or more of the seven key components that make up the body: food juice, blood, flesh, fat, bone, marrow, and semen (women too are said to have semen). Diet, climatic change, and mental attitude are thought to be important factors that can create disequilibrium between people and their environments and hence ill-health.

In Ayurvedic health care, diagnosis usually involves a detailed examination of the pulses as well as considerable intuition on the part of the practitioner. Therapy, which may involve the application of herbal remedies, changes in lifestyle and diet, or meditation, aims to restore the overall balance between the three humours and hence return the individual to good health.

## Chinese explanations

Traditional Chinese health care is also informed by holistic principles similar to those discussed above. The origins of these principles can be traced back thousands of years, at least as far as the *I Ching* or Book of Changes. This offers advice in the form of a series of metaphors, enabling those who consult it to gain insight into the relationship between themselves and the universe. Other writings that inform traditional Chinese health care include *The Yellow Emperor's Classic of Internal Medicine*, written about 200 BC, the *Materia Medica of Shennung* and *Important Prescriptions Worth Treasuring in the Golden Chamber*, both written about AD 200.

Traditional Chinese explanations of health, disease, and illness emphasize once again the relationship between people and their environments. In contrast to Ayurvedic thought in which there are three humours, in Chinese medicine there are six. These derive from fundamental life energy of *ch'i* as it is usually called. According to the teachings of traditional Chinese medicine, there is a constant interaction and exchange of energy between each person and the universe. Many of these interactions are rhythmical, following the natural cycles of the sun, moon, and seasons, and help establish a particular balance between two opposing energies in the body – *yin* and *yang*. Harmony between the cycles of the individual and those of the universe is essential for health and well-being.

Ch'i or life-force flows through the body via a number of *sinarteries* and can manifest itself in a variety of ways – as *ching*, a fundamental source of energy; as *shen*, which shapes the individual's character; as *p'o*, which moulds their personality; and as *hun*, which provides a stability for their psychic functions. Sinarteries cannot be seen in the same way as veins and arteries, and are perhaps best likened to lines of magnetic force. Disease is said to result from events that slow down or interrupt the flow of ch'i throughout the body. Some of these events may reside within the individual in the form of emotions such as anger, grief, worry, sorrow, and fear. Others, such as climatic conditions and warmth and cold, may be external to the person.

Diagnosis is usually carried out holistically, with attention being focused on different body parts and orifices, which may be touched, inspected, and smelled. In addition, a detailed case history may be taken of recent life events and of the relationship between these events and other environmental cycles. Therapy may involve acupuncture, massage, and moxybustion (the application of the burning ash of the mugwort plant) in an effort to ensure that energy flows freely again throughout the body.

*Early European explanations*

Until the beginning of the nineteenth century European explanations of health, disease, and illness were considerably influenced by Greek ideas developed as early as the fifth century BC. According to Greek physicians such as Empedocles and Hippocrates, health occurred when there was balance between four basic humours: blood, phlegm, yellow bile, and black bile. Later, these four humours were believed to be associated with four types of personality: the sanguine, the phlegmatic, the choleric, and the melancholic. An excess of any one of them led to sickness, the form this took being determined by the humour that was out of balance; thus an excess of black bile would be likely to lead to melancholia (Turner 1987).

Under this system, the task of the health specialist was to

work out which of the four humours was out of balance and then intervene to restore equilibrium. Changes in diet, exercise, and rest were often prescribed, as was bleeding, particularly in the case of fever. External factors such as climate and the individual's life-style and profession were also felt to affect health, but no matter what the cause of imbalance between the bodily humours, the overall emphasis in health care was on restoring an equilibrium between individuals and their environments.

In the second century AD, and under Roman influnce, ideas like these were refincd by the physician Galen. He believed that an excess of mucus caused illnesses in which the person was damp and cold, an excess of blood caused illnesses in which they were damp and hot, an excess of yellow bile caused those in which they were dry and hot, and an excess of black bile caused those in which they were dry and cold. Additionally, Galen believed that 'hot' diseases were best treated by 'cold' remedies, 'dry' ones by 'moist' remedies, and so on (Krieger 1981).

With the spread of Christianity, these beliefs changed, and early Christian beliefs came to overlay Galenic teaching. The New Testament mentions three causes of illness: the demons of possession, the sinning of individuals or their ancestors against God's commandments, and acts of God stemming from his omnipotence. It also advocates exorcism, prayer, fasting, and the laying on of hands as therapeutic procedures by which people can benefit from God's healing powers (Unschuld 1986). Teaching like this fitted uneasily with theories of humoral imbalance, and until the nineteenth century, Galenic and Christian ideas about health and illness co-existed in tension with one another. As Paul Unschuld puts it:

We can deduce from the statements made by various Christian authors who opposed the use of medicines based on the Hippocratic–Galenic essence theories, that they were aware of the threat posed by concepts of natural science to the spread of the Christian faith. Knowledge of the causes of illness as a result of pathogenic, climatic, emotional or dietary conditions contradicted biblical tradition concerning the links between sinful behaviour and being ill. It therefore called into question the need to follow the Christian ethic in order to prevent illness. This was a motive force that must not be underestimated.

(Unschuld 1986: 64)

From the Middle Ages onwards, professional health care in Europe was organized on the principle of what Norman Jewson (1976) has called *Bedside Medicine*. Under this system, health care was generally reserved for times of sickness rather than health, with the physicians making their diagnosis and recommending appropriate interventions, paying regard to the total condition of the patients, their present circumstances as well as their past history. In the popular and folk arenas (p. 5), on the other hand, health care was often provided by other household members as well as by those who had special 'knowledge' and 'powers' – conjurors, blessors, charmers, and purveyors of herbs and potions (Thomas 1971).

Continuing conflict between Galenic and Christian teaching about health led the church to denounce the publication of the first anatomy textbook by Vesalius in 1543. It also led many European explanations of health to assume a high moral tone. Thus by 1558, Luigi Cornaro was able to recommend the avoidance of meat, wine, and rich food as part of a diet which would not only safeguard against ill health but also protect against the temptations of the flesh. Similarly by the nineteenth century, ministers in the evangelical movement were recommending a plain and frugal diet, temperance, exercise, and a regular pattern of sleep as the lifestyle that would offer the best balance between physical health and Christian well-being (Turner 1982, 1987).

The publication of René Descartes' *Treatise on Man* in the seventeenth century was one of a number of factors which prepared the way for the development of modern bio-medicine. In contrast to the dominant view at the time, which saw everything in nature as the manifestation of God's will, Descartes' philosophy drew a distinction between the spiritual world and the material world. The material world and all it contained, including the human body could, he believed, be likened to a vast machine. It could thus be analysed by examining the form and function of each of its component parts.

These notions were strongly resisted at first since they ran contrary to Christian dogma, but they encouraged a growth of interest in the dissection of the human body. By 1628 William Harvey had established the workings of the heart and the circulatory system and other discoveries were soon to follow. This 'opening up of a few corpses', as Michel Foucault (1974: 51) has put it, was to have far-reaching consequences in that it allowed tissues and organs to be distinguished from one another. As a result, disease or pathology could now be *localized* within the body. It also prepared the ground for a new way of seeing the person. The bio-medical way of looking at things, or *gaze* as Michel Foucault calls it, gave scientific observation a key role in European health care practices. It also allowed the discoveries of doctors to assume a higher status than hitherto. Hereafter, they took the form of revelations or *positive truths*, rather than interpretative accounts of the nature of health problems

## Activities

Some of the health-care activities so far described have modern counterparts in alternative or complementary medicine.

1  Sharing the work amongst students in your group, find out all you can about the following alternative or complementary health care practices, their cultural and historical origins, and the ideas that underlie them. Use the library, local contacts, and perhaps talk to someone involved. Ask

your tutor for advice on how to go about this, bearing in mind the time available to you.

2 When you have collected your data, make a notice-board display which includes all the information you have come up with. Present the information on your display to others in your group.

- acupuncture
- aromatherapy
- reflexology
- homoeopathy
- chiropractic
- psychic healing

---

## Modern explanations of health, disease, and illness

Modern-day explanations of health can be classified into those which emphasize biological factors affecting people's health and those which emphasize social considerations. It is important to recognize, however, that modern theories differ from one another not so much in terms of whether they focus on *either* biological *or* social factors, but in accordance with the *relative weight* they give to each.

The majority of biological explanations are positivist in their approach, in that they have been developed using the methods and techniques of natural science. Some social explanations have been developed in a similar way. These are usually referred to as social-positivist explanations. On the other hand, there are also a number of very different social explanations around. Some of these have been developed by interactionist sociologists, whereas others have been developed by those who favour structuralist modes of explanations. In this section we shall briefly examine each of these more modern approaches in turn. Later, we will return to a more detailed consideration of social-positivist, interactionist, and structuralist theories about health.

*Bio-medical positivist explanations*

Towards the end of the eighteenth century, a major change took place in the organization and provision of health care in Europe. The transformation first began in France in response to demands for better health care from the poor, but it soon spread to other countries. Hitherto, in times of sickness and disease, health care had for the most part been provided within the home by household members and non-professionals as well as by physicians. The early 1800s, however, saw the growth of what Norman Jewson (1976) calls *hospital medicine*, as institutions were created in which the sick could be administered to on a grander scale. For most people, these early hospitals were not places to be visited by choice, rather they catered for the homeless and those who could not afford to be looked after at home. For doctors though, they provided a ready supply of research material (Waddington 1973) and this, together with development of *positivist* research techniques by natural scientists, led to the emergence of biomedicine as it is known today.

Positivism is a view of the world which suggests that the most important things around us are those which are observable and measurable, and positivist researchers are those who believe that by careful observation it is possible to identify the relationships between observable and measurable things. The relationships they are particularly interested in are those in which one variable can be said to cause another one – *cause and effect* relationships as they are generally known.

In the natural science, positivists go about their work by observing events, by noting what preceded them, and by identifying what follows them. They begin from tentative ideas or *hypotheses* about the relationship between variables and they then repeatedly *test* these ideas against the available evidence. This process of testing, and the observations that are made from it, eventually leads to the development of *theories* about the ways in which variables are related to one another.

Ideas such as these very much influenced the work of nineteenth- and twentieth-century European doctors. The observation and the dissection of corpses, for example, led physicians to locate disorders and pathologies within particular organs. It also encouraged the development of medical specialisms such as dermatology (skin), neurology (nervous system), obstetrics (childbirth), cardiology (heart), and haematology (blood), each of which focuses on a particular part of the body or a particular system within it. Because of this emphasis, bio-medical positivism came to concern itself largely with the presence of disease and illness, working from negative rather than positive definitions of health (see pp. 6–12).

Positivist inquiry also led to the development of new ideas about the origins of diseases. The doctrine of *specific etiology*, as it came to be called, suggested that specific diseases have specific causes, and it identified a key role for germs such as bacteria and viruses in this process. Prior to this, it had been widely believed that one cause could give rise to many different diseases. Thus miasma, or bad air, was thought to be responsible for diseases as diverse as cholera, typhus, measles, bronchitis, and pneumonia. Finally, positivist bio-medical thought led to the widespread adoption of *allopathic* kinds of treatment, which use drugs as a kind of 'antidote' for the diseases they are used to treat.

To summarize, bio-medical positivism suggests that illness or distress arises from a malfunction in some part of the body, that malfunctions can be detected by appropriately trained experts using appropriate scientific aids, and that once detected, malfunctions can usually be treated by administering drugs or by removing or surgically modifying the part of the body that is no longer working properly (Open University 1985b).

The scientific medicine, to which bio-medical positivism gave rise, is far from a neutral activity. Indeed, it has had wide-ranging social consequences. According to Lesley Doyal and Imogen Pennell (1979: 30), it is 'curative, individualistic and interventionist', it objectifies patients, and it denies 'their status as social beings'. No matter what doctors working within this tradition may say to the opposite, people in their wholeness are rarely the subject of the medical interest in the way that they are with other systems of health care. Instead, diseased organs and unbalanced physiological systems become the major focus of medical attention.

## Activities

1 Think back to the last time you visited the doctor for a minor health problem. Make a note of this problem.
2 Now think about the questions you were asked by the doctor. Did they focus on the one particular aspect of your health, or did they take the form of more general questions about your overall well-being? Make a note of these too.
3 Next, think about the examination that took place. Did this focus on one part of your body or on a restricted number of parts, or were you examined from top to toe? Make a note of how the examination took place.
4 Share your experiences with others in small groups and ask someone to keep a record of the discussion. Remember, there is no need to reveal anything you feel embarrassed about.
5 Finally, discuss the following questions.
   • What do your experiences tell you about the focus of modern bio-medicine?
   • Is this focus on the person as a whole or on a part of them?
   • Are all doctors the same in the focus they adopt?
   • How could we go about investigating these issues more systematically?

## Social-positivist explanations

As techniques for identifying disease became more sophisticated, it became clear that while many people had been exposed to virulent bacteria and viruses, only a few of them became ill as a result. Some developed an immunity to particular micro-organisms, in many cases without realizing that they had been infected. Others did not become infected at all in circumstances where this might have been expected. At first, findings like these were hard to explain. As Nicky Hart has put it, why does disease seem to be rare when infection is often the norm? (Hart 1985: 15). *Germ theory* which bio-medical positivism had helped develop offered little guidance on this matter. Even harder to explain was why mortality from infectious disease had been falling for several decades *before* micro-organisms were first identified (Figure 9). And why, when bacteria and viruses were known about, did this new knowledge seem to have little effect on the rate of decline in mortality? Evidence like this pointed to the existence of factors other than those of a purely biological nature that

Figure 9  *Mean annual mortality rate from respiratory tuberculosis, England and Wales, 1838–1982*

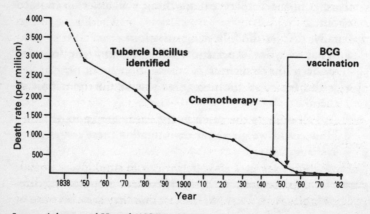

*Source*: Acheson and Hagard (1984) p. 14

affected health and well-being. As a result, attention became increasingly focused on the social causes of disease, be they an individual's knowledge, attitudes, and behaviour with respect to health matters, be they particular ways of living, or be they environmental factors.

Even hard-line adherents of bio-medical positivism will acknowledge, when pushed, that social factors can be causes of health, disease, and illness. Where they differ from others working in the health field lies in the emphasis they give to these. Bio-medical positivists, for example, often suggest that social factors may be important only in certain circumstances and for certain individuals. Social positivists, on the other hand, argue that while there is a biological basis for health and disease, social influences have an important role to play across a wide range of situations. Their inquiries have led them to identify a variety of social factors affecting health. These factors can be divided into three main types: life-style variables, cultural influences, and environmental factors.

*Life-style* variables are factors to do with individual social behaviour. They may include smoking habits, patterns of alcohol consumption, and dietary preferences. In many social-positivist accounts, the assumption is often made that variables like these are under the direct control of the individuals concerned. That is people can choose whether or not to smoke, whether or not to eat healthily, or whether or not to take regular exercise. Life-style variables are often cited by politicians and by some health educators as the key to a healthier society. All that people need is information about how to live more healthily for them to be able to make the right choices.

## Activities

Table 6 shows sex and class variations in smoking. A social-positivist explanation of these differences emphasizing life-style variables would tend to suggest that they arise because of the *choices* people make.

1 Write down some of the factors that you think might influence
  ● women's 'decisions' whether or not to smoke
  ● men's 'decisions' whether or not to smoke
  ● people of different occupational backgrounds' 'decisions' whether or not to smoke.
2 Using this evidence, hold a debate on the topic 'People who die from lung cancer through smoking only have themselves to blame because they decided to smoke in the first place'.
3 Make a list of the points that can be used to support the view that the people freely decide whether or not to smoke and those that question it.

Table 6  *Prevalence of cigarette smoking in Britain, 1972 and 1984, by sex and occupational background (% smoking cigarettes)*

|  | Occupational background | | | | | |
|  | I | II | IIIN | IIIM | IV | V |
|---|---|---|---|---|---|---|
| *Women* | | | | | | |
| 1972 | 33 | 38 | 38 | 47 | 42 | 42 |
| 1984 | 15 | 29 | 28 | 37 | 37 | 36 |
| *Men* | | | | | | |
| 1972 | 33 | 44 | 45 | 57 | 57 | 64 |
| 1984 | 17 | 29 | 30 | 40 | 45 | 49 |

*Source*: OPCS (1986)

*Cultural influences*, on the other hand, are those that are said to influence groups of individuals who share a common background. They arise from the shared norms and values existing within a neighbourhood or community. These make it seem sensible to adopt particular courses of action on health matters and to refrain from others. For example, local traditions may encourage some people to consume food that is unhealthy for them, others may discourage regular visits to the doctors or the dentist, yet others may advocate poor child-rearing practices, which have serious long-term consequences for the health of the child.

Because of their focus on the individual and the community of which she or he is a part, explanations of health, disease, and illness which emphasize life-styles and/or cultural influences are often described as *individualistic* in their stance. They are also sometimes described as *victim-blaming* theories, since they tend to imply that people only have themselves to blame if they become ill (Graham 1985). It will come as little surprise, therefore, to learn that historically they have tended to be associated with self-help and with the view that the state can do little to remedy the fundamental causes of ill-health which reside in the decisions individuals make.

Social-positivist explanations have also identified *environmental factors* at home and at work as social determinants of health, but ones which are relatively beyond the control of individuals. At home, these include overcrowding and lack of privacy. At work, factors such as temperature, light, dust, fumes, and noise, themselves the result of the way in which the work environment has been organized, can have a powerful effect on health and well-being. So can more obviously psychological factors such as whether people are encouraged to work alone or in small groups. More generally environmental pollution by wastes, nuclear radiation, and industrial by-products can have serious consequences for health. When considering health hazards such as these, however, it is important to identify the *social processes* that have led to particular environmental factors becoming the threats they are.

Finally, it is important to recognize that social positivists, like their bio-medical counterparts, tend to define health negatively. It should therefore come as little surprise to discover that most of their research has been concerned with identifying the social factors responsible for disease.

67

## Interactionist explanations

In contrast to positivists, who are often interested in identifying external influences affecting health, interactionist sociologists as their name suggests tend to be more interested in studying the interaction between these events and interpretative processes. For them, the most important quality that people possess is their ability to interact with one another in ways that are meaningful. Women and men are essentially *meaning-givers* who construct understandings of themselves and others out of the experiences they have and the relationships they enter into. Herbert Blumer (1969) identifies three key starting-points for most interactionist accounts:

1 People act on the basis of meanings.
2 Meanings arise from interaction with others, especially interaction with intimate others.
3 The meanings that people, objects, and situations have are not fixed but are continuously modified in the light of new experience.

When it comes to explaining health, these ideas raise a series of important questions. In particular, they focus attention on the processes by which people come to understand themselves as healthy or not. According to interactionists, individuals *actively construct* understandings of themselves using the evidence that comes from their interactions with others. Some of these interactions may lead them to understand themselves as healthy. Others may have the opposite effect, leading the person concerned to feel that they are ill. According to this perspective, the reactions of others are vital in helping us make decisions about matters like these.

To illustrate what is meant by this, imagine that you wake up one morning feeling slightly under the weather. You may decide to keep this information to yourself, deciding that there is nothing really the matter. Alternatively you might decide to share the information with other people. Depending on their reactions, you may or may not decide you are seriously ill. Imagine how you would feel if, on hearing the news, your best friend said, 'Now you've mentioned it, you've looked really ill for weeks'. Think now how you would feel if they said, 'Oh forget about it, it's probably nothing, just too many late nights, that's all'. Both of these reactions could easily be triggered off by exactly the same evidence, your comment about not feeling too well, but each could have very different consequences for how you subsequently feel about yourself.

Of course on some occasions people may find that their actions are *labelled* for them – as signs of sickness or disease. Throughout history, many kinds of statistically unusual behaviour have been reacted to in this way, and doctors, psychologists, teachers, the police, and the judiciary have a key role to play in this process. But to say that someone (or their behaviour) is 'sick', 'ill', 'mad', or 'diseased' may also be to confirm the individual in that identity. People react to the labels they are given in many different ways, but for a sizeable number of individuals they may easily become *self-fulfilling prophesies* – identities to be lived up to in future interactions with others.

Furthermore when it comes to labelling, some people are more powerful than others. Thus if an educational psychologist tells a parent that her daughter is 'hyperactive' or if a doctor tells a patient that he has a 'kidney problem', the effects of this labelling are usually more serious than if these same judgements were made by the local car park attendant. Labelling is therefore a process which involves the use of *power*. Sometimes labels may be successfully resisted by those to whom they are applied. On other occasions, this may be much more difficult.

In contrast to bio-medical and social positivist researchers, interactionists tend to focus on the more subjective aspects of health. Their interest lies in the experiences people have and the self-understandings that develop from these. Many of their studies therefore look at what it means to be healthy and what it means to be ill. Their inquiries therefore encompass both positive and negative definitions of health.

## Structuralist explanations

In their desire to do justice to the way in which people actively construct meanings out of the situations they find themselves in, interactionist accounts face a series of problems. First, they fail to specify the limits to the ways in which people can come to understand their health status. As we shall see in Chapter 5, some interactionist accounts almost imply that health is all in the mind, and that all that someone has to do in order to be healthy is to think that way. Second, they have little to say about the broader social context which surrounds individuals and the way in which it influences health. Both of these issues are taken up by structuralist explanations.

Structuralist explanations have their origins in the fact that disease and illness do not strike individuals at random. Rather, health is patterned or *structured* within countries and between them, with some groups coming out consistently better no matter what measure of health is chosen (see Chapter 2). This prompts us to question what causes these patterns, and structuralist sociologists believe that there is something about the way in which society as a whole is organized that influences them.

As we will see later, there are many different points of view within structuralist thought. By far the most influential accounts, however, have been developed by Marxist sociologists. According to them, the starting-point for an adequate explanation of health inequalities must be an understanding of the nature of capitalist economic systems. While these may differ in detail from one another, they are similar in that they give rise to major economic inequalities between those who own the means of production (the capitalists) and those who sell their labour for wages (the working class). These economic inequalities in turn create inequalities in health. For example, production for profit often results in dangerous and health-threatening work conditions for working-class people employed in factories. Additionally the inherent instability of capitalist economies, with their tendency to fluctuate between 'booms' and 'slumps', means high levels of unemployment from time to time, with their associated health risks. Capitalism also requires a sufficiently healthy and disciplined work-force to ensure that production takes place uninterrupted. However, it is rarely in the interests of capitalists to provide health care themselves. Rather, in advanced capitalist societies, the state and the households in which individuals live take on this role, with variable success (Navarro 1976). All of these factors combine to produce the health inequalities between classes that we have already seen, as well as those between other social groups.

As we shall see in Chapter 6, structuralist explanations of health are not only concerned with the origins of health inequalities, but also with how these change over time. In order to do this, they raise important questions about dominant understandings of health, the role of doctors in society, the impact of the profit motive on standards of health care, and the relationship between multinational drugs companies and their clients (Waitzkin and Waterman 1974).

In recent years, another strand of structuralist analysis has developed which focuses particularly on the health experiences of women. Using historical evidence, feminist sociologists have begun to develop analyses of the ways in which patriarchy (male power) has structured women's health experience. Particular attention has been given to the various ways in which women's sexuality has been subjected to patriarchal control (Laws 1985; Pollock 1985) childbirth has been medicalized (Oakley 1984), and women's psychology presented as intrinsically unstable and abnormal (Ehrenreich and English 1978; Showalter 1987; Penfold and Walker 1984). To these and other related issues we shall return later.

## Activities

1  Allocate the following explanations to one of the following types: traditional, bio-medical positivist, social-positivist,

interactionist, structuralist. Find supporting statements from this chapter to back up the decisions you make.

2 Discuss your views with others and with your tutor. Be ready to justify any conclusions you reach.

3 If you have time, make up some additional explanations to fit each type and see whether other members of your group agree with them.

- At the age of 72, Gwen developed pneumonia because of her poor housing conditions.
- Penny decided to take a day off work sick because it seemed the most sensible thing to do in the circumstances.
- Jillie's passion for aerobics led her to attend class every day until a cartilage injury meant that she had to take things easy for a while.
- Matthew had to spend a couple of days in bed after developing a streptococcal throat infection.
- Paula, Jean, and other women in the office never felt better in their lives than they did the day they won their case for sexual harassment against Ray the Sales Manager.
- In the end, Terry's love of drink and cigarettes got the better of him. After being admitted to hospital, he was diagnosed with cancer of the mouth and throat.
- In order to keep their profits up, the company neglected to replace the old piping around the chemical processor. Eventually a seal gave way and Keith and four other employees died after being overcome by fumes.

*Further reading*

*If you are interested in finding out more about traditional explanations of health, chapters 1 and 2 in Stacey (1988) are a good starting-point. Social positivism in its various forms underpins much of George Brown's discussion in chapter 9 of Tuckett (1976). Chapter 10 in Tuckett (1976), written by*

*David Field, discusses some of the early work carried out by interactionists. Chapter 1 of Doyal and Pennell (1979) offers an overview of modern explanations of health, disease, and illness with a particular emphasis on Marxist accounts. Further reading on social-positivist, interactionist, and structuralist explanations can be found at the end of Chapters 4, 5, and 6 in this volume.*

# 4

# *Social-positivist explanations*

So far, we have looked at a variety of ways in which health can be defined, a number of techniques that can be used to measure it, and some of the different ways in which it can be explained. In doing this, we have distinguished between those explanations which have a biological focus and those which suggest that social factors have a significant role to play in determining health. In the remainder of this book, attention will be focused on several different social explanations. In this chapter, the emphasis will be on those that are broadly *social-positivist* in their emphasis. In subsequent chapters, inter-actionist and structuralist explanations will be looked at in more detail.

## The logic of positivist inquiry

In general terms, positivist researchers attempt to apply the logic and methods of the natural sciences to the study of social events and social situations. They do this because they believe that the social world of people and relationships, just like the world of inanimate objects, has regular and predictable features ready to be discovered by those who seek them out (see pp. 61–6). Thus social positivists look for the causes of ill-health in the social context, whereas bio-medical positivists look for causes in micro-organisms and in anatomical and physiological abnormalities.

Most positivists therefore begin their work by observing events and classifying them into categories. Indeed, this process of classification is 'the first and most indispensable condition of all proofs and verifications' since a later theory 'can only be checked if we know how to recognize the facts of which it is intended to give an account' (Durkheim 1966: 34). However, it is the relationship between categories or variables that positivists are particularly interested in. These can often be established by putting preliminary ideas about them (or hypotheses) to the test. A logical series of steps needs to be followed in testing hypotheses.

For example, take the two variables 'poor lighting' and 'having a headache'. If a researcher has hypothesized that working in a poorly lit room causes headaches, and if she wishes to investigate this hypothesis further, she must first specify the nature of the relationship between these two variables. In so doing, she may need to consider, for example, whether she believes that poor lighting simply triggers off a headache, or whether she believes there is an association between the quality of the lighting and the intensity of the headache, such that the dimmer the light the worse the headache is likely to be. She will also need to consider whether the hypothesized relationship holds true for all kinds of work or whether it relates only to activities of particular kinds.

Having given thought to this, the next problem is that of operationalizing each variable. This involves identifying suitable indicators of lighting and headache intensity. The first of these may be relatively easy to quantify with a light meter similar to those used by photographers, but the second may cause greater problems.

Assuming it is possible to deal with these difficulties, situations now either have to be found, or to be specially created, in which the hypothesized relationship ought to be present. In the case of this example, a number of naturally occurring situations could be identified in which a group of comparable individuals work on the same task under different lighting intensities, e.g. students in different parts of a library. Alternatively it might be possible to collect data in a controlled laboratory setting. There would be strengths and weaknesses associated with testing the hypothesized relationship in each of these environments, and some overall assessment of the relative merits of the two contexts will have to be made before data collection can proceed.

Finally, data will need to be collected in each of these situations and the relationship between the variables quantified. In the light of this assessment, the researcher may conclude *either* that there is no evidence for the hypothesized relationship *or* that there is some evidence for this relationship.

## Activities

A widely held lay health belief suggests that going swimming after a meal gives you stomach cramps.

Working in small groups, plan a small-scale social-positivist study to investigate the accuracy of this belief. Use the following questions to help you do this.

- What are the key variables in the study?
- What is the hypothesized relationship between these variables?
- What would be suitable indicators of these variables?
- What kinds of situations need to be investigated?
- Will data be collected in natural settings or in more controlled environments?
- What observations will need to be made?

When carrying out an inquiry like this, care needs to be taken to ensure that variables other than those that are of interest do not interfere with the study. In the case of research into the relationship between lighting intensity and headaches, for example, we would want to be sure that all other factors that might plausibly cause headaches (such as noise, tiredness, or the previous consumption of alcohol) are carefully *controlled* throughout the investigation. If they are not, then an effect which we might believe to be caused by lighting intensity may in fact be caused by one of these outside influences.

In the case of a laboratory study, it may be possible to control variables in this way, but in the real world, it is very difficult to do this. To make matters more complicated, however, when it comes to explaining social behaviour, not one but many factors may need to be taken into account. Rarely are social positivist researchers interested in *monocausal* explanations. Instead, they often seek to develop *multivariate analyses* of events. These specify the ways in which a number of variables combine together to produce particular outcomes (see pp. 27–9). Durkheim's work on suicide is the classic example of this latter approach (Durkheim 1970) and since then, social positivists have tried to use similar research techniques to investigate a wide range of health issues.

## Identifying causal influences

One of the great strengths of social positivism lies in its potential to identify the causes of ill-health. However, deciding whether a particular variable is a causal influence is often far from straightforward. David Armstrong (1983) has identified three conditions which must be met before we can decide that two variables are causally related.

First, the variables must be in the correct temporal sequence. The variable which is believed to be the cause must precede the one which it is predicted to affect. Thus if we hypothesize that job loss is a cause of anxiety and depression, the situations we must study are those in which job loss occurs first of all.

Second, there must be a correlation between the variables that are believed to be related. As one varies, so should the other. Correlations can be of different kinds. For example, there are positive correlations where, as one variable increases, so does the other. Two variables which show this kind of relationship are exercise and muscle tone – the more exercise you take, the firmer your muscles will be. Then there are negative correlations where as one variable increases, the other decreases. An illustration of this kind of relationship could be provided by a study looking at the relationship between relaxation therapy and anxiety. Generally speaking, the more someone practises relaxation exercises, the less anxious they are likely to feel.

Third, there must be no hidden third variables causing both of the variables we are interested in to change. As an illustration of this, we can consider the case of alcohol consumption and liver damage. At first sight, the relationship here seems quite straightforward. According to many studies there is a correlation between alcohol consumption and cirrhosis of the liver. What is more, the temporal sequence of these two events is usually clear cut, with alcohol consumption preceding liver damage in those affected. However, before we can conclude that alcohol causes liver damage, we have to rule out the possibility that there are no hidden third variables such as personality factors or stress which cause *both* high alcohol consumption *and* liver damage. This is often hard to do.

Things are further complicated by the fact that rarely is there one cause of ill-health. Indeed according to social positivist analyses, causal influences are usually chained together into sequences. Thus, a number of social factors may interact with one another to render the individual more susceptible to disease. Thus unemployment may lead to poverty, which may in turn result in poor housing and a poor diet. These two factors may then combine to make it more

78

likely that the individual will develop serious physical or mental illness.

## Epidemiology and social positivism

Epidemiologists have a key role to play in identifying the social factors affecting health. Four main techniques are employed in their work.

### Descriptive studies

In descriptive studies, epidemiologists record the incidence of illness or disease in different populations. They may compare the rates of disease or illness in different countries, different regions, and different groups. For example, their focus may be on the incidence of a particular complaint amongst women compared with men. On other occasions, age or occupational background may be the key variable they are interested in. This kind of research alone lends itself to identifying trends in the incidence of illness and disease. We have already come across research of this kind in Chapter 2, where variations in morbidity were analysed on the basis of occupational background, sex, age, and ethnicity.

### Case-control studies

Case-control studies are those in which the epidemiologist compares members of a given social group who have the illness or disease (the cases) with others from the same group without it (the controls). They are thus a kind of retrospective experiment. In this sort of research, it is important to ensure that the two groups have indeed been drawn from the same population. Only by doing this will it be possible to identify the key factors that distinguish the cases from the controls. This particular technique led researchers to identify some of the factors responsible for the transmission of HIV infection in the early 1980s. Amongst injecting drug users, for example, it was found that those who shared needles and syringes were more likely to acquire the infection than others. This led to the conclusion that in so far as the risk of HIV is concerned, it is not whether you inject drugs that matters but *how* injection takes place. Provided sterile equipment is used on every occasion, and provided syringes and needles are not shared, HIV is not transmitted by this route.

## Cohort studies

In cohort studies, data are collected from matched groups of individuals. These differ from one another, however, in terms of a key variable which it is hypothesized might be the cause of the disease or illness under investigation. Thus in studying lung cancer, a cohort of smokers might be compared with a group of non-smokers matched on the basis of sex, occupational background, race, and age to determine whether or not smoking might plausibly be identified as a cause of the disease.

## Migrant studies

In migrant studies, the incidence of a particular complaint is studied amongst members of a group who have moved from one part of the world to another, amongst members of the community they left, and amongst members of the community they joined. By obtaining data in these three settings, it is possible to identify the causes of illness and disease. Migrant studies have proved particularly successful in enabling researchers to distinguish between the genetic and social determinants of ill-health. For example, the low incidence of breast cancer amongst women living in Japan compared with the USA was originally taken as support for the view that some groups might be genetically protected against this form of disease. Subsequent research, however, has disproved this initial hypothesis since the incidence of breast cancer amongst Japanese women living in the USA has risen steadily over successive generations to equal the overall US rate.

## The outcomes of social-positivist inquiry

In Chapter 3 an important distinction was drawn between three types of social-positivist explanation: those that emphasize life-style variables, those that focus on cultural influences, and those that identify the environmental determinants of health. It is important to recognize, however, that these descriptions identify broad types of explanation which overlap with one another. As we will see when it comes to examining particular pieces of research carried out within a social-positivist framework, the causal mechanisms identified within them may make reference to each of these different but related kinds of influence. Here, we shall briefly consider a number of key areas of research that have been influenced by each of these broad approaches.

### Life-style variables

Life-style variables are factors to do with individual behaviour, though it is important to recognize that such behaviour can still be shown to follow the norms of different social groups. Some of the more familiar life-style variables affecting health include dietary preferences such as the amount of sugar consumed, exercise patterns such as the amount of regular physical activity undertaken, drinking choices such as the quantity of alcohol drunk, and patterns of sexual behaviour such as the extent to which an individual places himself or herself, or indeed his or her partner, at risk of sexually transmitted infection. Many, if not all, of these factors are popularly believed to be under the direct control of individuals. Whether, or how far, this is true is of course a different matter (see pp. 70–1).

In recent years a considerable amount of time has been given over to studying variables such as these and the effects they may have on health. Nowhere is this clearer than in the study of smoking and its consequences. For over thirty years a link between smoking and lung disease has been suspected, and for at least twenty years there has been strong evidence to support such a claim. In Britain, much of this has come from the work of Richard Doll and his colleagues, who have carried out longitudinal studies of patterns of tobacco use and deaths from lung cancer. Some of their work has looked at patterns in the population as a whole, whereas other parts of it have focused on specific occupational groups. In particular, their study of over 30,000 doctors enabled them to compare lung cancer rates for smokers compared with non-smokers and for those who gave up smoking in response to health education compared with those who continued. This work showed convincingly that not only is smoking a cause of lung cancer, but also in Britain it contributes significantly to deaths from bronchitis and heart disease (Doll and Peto 1976).

## Cultural influences

Research into the cultural influences affecting health has a long history. It has underpinned much of the cross-cultural research carried out by medical anthropologists who have examined cultural beliefs and aspirations, the social practices to which these give rise, and patterns of illness and disease. As David Mechanic puts it:

> The culture of a group affects every aspect of growth and development, the acquisition of goals and aspirations, the risk factors to which one is exposed and modes of response and adaptation. ... It is a truism that the health of a people reflects the way it chooses to live, but it remains a point of great significance.
>
> (Mechanic 1978: 56–7)

In Britain the dominant view throughout the nineteenth century, challenged only by social reformers such as Edwin Chadwick (author of the 1842 *Report on the Sanitary*

*Conditions of the Labouring Classes of Great Britain*) and Sidney and Beatrice Webb, held that much of the ill-health experienced by working-class families could be explained in terms of cultural factors. Ignorance, negligence, or pure fecklessness were perceived as the cause of the problem and these qualities were believed to be easily transmitted from one generation to the next. Frequently women were singled out for special blame. As George Newman, Chief Medical Officer at the Board of Education, put it in 1906:

> The problem of infant mortality is not one of sanitation alone, or housing or, indeed, of poverty as such, but is mainly a question of motherhood ... death in infancy is probably more due to such ignorance and negligence than any other cause, as becomes evident when we remember that epidemic diarrhoea, convulsive debility and atrophy which are among the most common causes of death, are brought about in large measure owing to improper feeding or ill-timed weaning; bronchitis and pneumonia are due not infrequently to careless exposure (indoor or outdoor); and death through measles or whooping cough is largely caused by mismanagement of nursing.
>
> (cited in Graham 1985: 28)

Ideas like these are still with us today. Writing in 1976, David Tuckett draws heavily upon the work of Willmott and Young (1962), Young and Willmott (1973), and Goldthorpe *et al.* (1969) to argue that clear-cut cultural differences can be established between working-class and middle-class homes. These, Tuckett believes, have important implications for health and well-being.

> For example, the fact that manual workers and their wives are less likely to plan their families by spacing births and the fact that the early years of their marital relationship are unlikely to be of the kind where the partners feel they can confide in each other about any kind of problem means that they are more vulnerable to depression following a life

crisis. Similarly, the fact that the perspectives of working class people do not emphasize individual action to secure future ends, offers one reason for working class parents being less likely to visit welfare clinics with their children or to take preventive action in relation to pre-natal or dental care.

(Tuckett 1976: 151)

Regardless of whether they have been developed from cross-cultural inquiry or from research within one particular society, cultural explanations feed readily into notions of deficit and deficiency in certain social groups. As a result, those who are culturally different come quickly to be seen as culturally and socially *deficient*.


## Environmental factors

In Chapter 3 an important distinction was drawn between two rather different kinds of environmental explanations: those that are positive in their emphasis and those that are more negative. The first of these two types of explanations points to the overall improvement in health that in many societies has accompanied industrialization. The second focuses attention on the less beneficial effects of industrial development: mechanization and its human consequences, urbanization and its social effects, and pollution and its possible long-term effects. Here, we will focus on one particular environmental explanation which is broadly positive in the claims it makes – that offered by Thomas McKeown (1976) to account for the steady decline in mortality that took place throughout Europe in the nineteenth and twentieth centuries.

The starting-point for McKeown's work lay in his attempts to explain the growth in the British population that took place throughout the nineteenth and into the twentieth century. This is shown in Figure 10. It will be noted that this growth was triggered off by an initial decline in the death-rate. This began in the late eighteenth century and continued until the

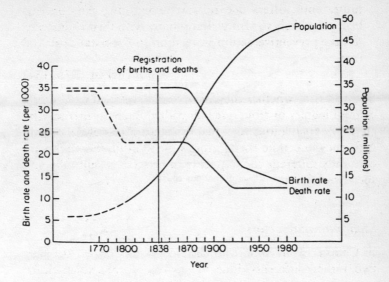

*Source*: Acheson and Hagard (1984) p. 12

late 1830s. Mortality then remained constant until the 1870s, when it began to fall again. Throughout this period the birth-rate remained constant, but this too began to fall in the late nineteenth century. This change from a high birth-rate and a high death-rate to a low birth-rate and a low death-rate is often referred to as a *demographic transition*.

McKeown was particularly interested in the factors responsible for the reduction in mortality over this period, and his inquiries led him to identify the decline of infectious disease as the main force at work (see Figure 11).

In the early 1800s tuberculosis, typhus, typhoid, scarlet fever, cholera, dysentery and, to a lesser extent, smallpox were major causes of mortality, but throughout the century their effects diminished. McKeown identifies three possible

Figure 11 *Mean annual death-rate from infectious and non-infectious causes, England and Wales, 1948–80*

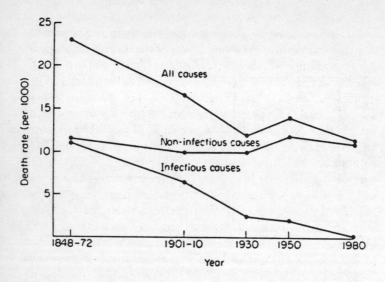

*Source*: Acheson and Hagard (1984) p. 12

reasons for this sustained decline in mortality due to infectious disease: (1) a spontaneous change in either the virulence of the infective micro-organisms or in the resistance of the host, (2) medical measures, and (3) changes in the environment. He examines each of these possible explanations in turn.

The first is rejected on the grounds that there is no evidence of significant mutations in the nature of the infective organisms responsible for these diseases over the period concerned, nor of an increased natural resistance to them in the host. McKeown rejects the second explanation too because mortality from these diseases was falling significantly well *before* the micro-organisms responsible for them were identified (see Figure 9). Moreover, it was not until the mid-twentieth century that effective drug therapy was developed against many of the infections concerned. Only in the case of small-pox, which was not a major contributor to mortality over the period concerned, is there evidence that vaccination played a role in reducing the incidence of infection.

McKeown therefore concludes that the main factor responsible for this decline in mortality was environmental change. In particular, improvements in agriculture and transport significantly affected the quantity and quality of food available. Many of these changes were brought about, not by advances in chemical and technological methods, but by 'an extension of traditional methods such as conversation of fertility, enclosure, crop rotation, winter feeding and extension of land under cultivation' (Acheson and Hagard 1984: 27). Towards the end of the nineteenth century, improvements in the water supply and in sewage disposal began to have an effect on mortality, but it was not until the mid-1930s that chemotherapy and vaccination became major determinants of an improved public health. In this respect, his work echoes that of René Dubos (1959), who also was sceptical of the claim that bio-medicine had contributed significantly to the decline in mortality throughout the nineteenth century.

In contrast to some of the other social-positivist studies reviewed, McKeown's work relies heavily on descriptive epidemiological research and careful historical analysis. McKeown died in June 1988, but he left a legacy which seriously questions many common-sense ideas about modern bio-medicine and its achievements. In particular, it asks us to consider carefully the interrelationship of social and biological factors as key determinants of health.

## The consequences of social-positivist inquiry

It would be inappropriate to end this chapter without considering briefly some of the broader consequences of social-positivist explanations of health – particularly in so far as they have had identifiable effects for the organization of health care in Europe and North America.

The first thing to be said is that social-positivist accounts call into question the ability of bio-medicine to explain all important health issues. By highlighting the role that life-style variables, cultural influences, and environmental factors can play in determining health, social-positivist research has identified whole realms of experience that are not amenable to explanation in purely bio-medical terms. As a result, there can be few health professionals nowadays whose beliefs and whose work is uninfluenced by social-positivist considerations. Nevertheless, the emphasis that is given to these concerns varies depending on the individual and the role they play in health care provision. Thus those employed in community health care and those working to prevent ill-health may find social-positivist findings more directly relevant than those employed in other settings.

Social-positivism is an acutely *individualistic* mode of explanation. It focuses attention on individuals and their life-styles, household units, and their health beliefs, and social groups and their cultures, and it does this at the expense of broader social determinants of health such as class, ethnicity, sex, and age. It is therefore far from neutral as an analysis since it singles out the individual and the relationships she or he has with others as key factors affecting health. As a result, the kinds of health care interventions which social-positivism encourages also tend to focus on individuals and their immediate surroundings. To some extent this may be reassuring, since it suggests that on a one-to-one basis there is much that can be done to alleviate ill-health. However, this kind of health care activity may leave unchallenged broader social forces influencing health inequalities.

Social-positivist analyses have also given rise to greater *specialization* and *professionalization* within health care. They are not, of course, the only forces responsible for this. In Chapter 3, for example, we saw that many kinds of traditional and modern health care have given rise to specialized roles and responsibilities. But the advent of social-positivist analysis has fuelled this tendency, such that in Europe and North

America there are now specialists in a wide range of environmental and community health issues. There is also an ever-growing league of health care professionals – community health specialists, health visitors, and district nurses – who are charged with the responsibility of intervening directly in people's lives around the supposed cultural, social, and environmental causes of ill-health.

Finally, Ivan Illich (1975) has detected in these processes of increased specialization and professionalization the seeds of three kinds of iatrogenesis, or damage created by medicine. The first of these, which he calls *clinical iatrogenesis*, has its origins in the, often unintended, consequences of treatment, and relates rather more closely to bio-medical considerations than the other two. The second and third types of iatrogenesis he talks about – social iatrogenesis and structural iatrogenesis – are more closely related to the development of health care influenced by social-positivist concerns. By *social iatrogenesis*, Illich is referring to the tendency for people to become addicted, mentally and emotionally, to medical care as a cure for all their problems, be they biological or social in nature. By *structural iatrogenesis*, Illich means the tendency for people to lose their capacity for autonomy in health matters and self-care. The origins of these three forms of damage can be found in the culture of industrialization and its suggestion that most human problems are merely technical issues that can readily be resolved with the right technology.

## Activities

Social-positivist ideas about health are fairly widespread in society, and statements by politicians, armchair commentators, and health professionals often rely heavily on them.

1 Working in groups of about four, select a popular news magazine and get hold of a couple of week's back copies (your local reference library may keep these).
2 Make a note of the stories that have been published on illness

and disease, and examine these carefully to identify the kinds of explanations that are given for the problems reported.

3 Make a list of quotes which identify social-positivist explanations. Check that everyone in your group agrees that the ones you have chosen have got this particular emphasis.

4 Present your quotations to the rest of the class and be prepared to justify the decisions you have reached using the information you have read about in this chapter.

*Further reading*

*Most basic sociology textbooks contain an introduction to positivist methodology. Chapter 12 in Bilton et al. (1987) offers an accessible account of the main issues. For a summary of the main features of Durkheim's work on* Suicide, *see chapter 3 in Aggleton (1987). For a more extended discussion of the issues see Taylor (1987).*

*Life-styles and cultural factors are emphasized in the section entitled 'Cultural/behavioural explanations' in chapter 6 of Townsend and Davidson (1982). Chapter 6 of Townsend et al. (1988) revisits some of these issues in the light of more recent evidence, and two sections in particular, 'Evidence on cultural/behavioural differences' and 'How much of the differential does life-style explain?' are worth reading.*

*There can be no substitute for reading McKeown's work in the original. Try McKeown (1976) or McKeown (1979). Chapter 2 in Acheson and Hagard (1984), which is in fact the third edition of McKeown and Lowe's textbook,* An Introduction to Social Medicine, *provides a good summary of the main issues. Illich (1975) deals in a challenging way with some of the negative consequences of modern medicine. Although it is sometimes hailed as a radical text, the remedies it suggests have been accused of romanticism, idealism, and individualism. Doyal and Pennell (1979) offer a summary and a critique of his main arguments on pages 17–20.*

# 5

# *Interactionist explanations*

In contrast to social-positivist researchers, who are keen to identify the social causes of ill-health and well-being, interactionists are more interested in what it means to be healthy, what it means to be diseased, and what it means to be ill. For them, the most basic human qualities are those associated with interaction, communication, and, above all, meaning-giving. People construct understandings of themselves and of others out of the experiences they have and the situations they find themselves in. These understandings have consequences in turn for the way in which people act, and the manner in which others react to them.

While the origins of social-positivism lie in attempts to apply natural science methodology to the study of behaviour, the origins of interactionism can be found in the writings of sociologists and philosophers who were either sceptical about or critical of the value of such an approach. At the end of the last century, writers such as Max Weber and Wilhelm Dilthey were influential in establishing the broadly *anti-positivistic* framework within which interactionism developed. In contrast to social-positivism, anti-positivist theory suggests that the origins of behaviour are not external to the individual. Rather, they reside within the person in the form of the understandings and meanings which make it 'sensible' and 'logical' to act in particular ways. The task of the sociologist, therefore, is to identify these meanings. Only by doing this will it be possible truly to understand human social behaviour.

This kind of perspective is very different from that discussed in Chapter 4 and calls for the use of new research techniques, ones which are sensitive to the quality, rather than the quantity of human experience.

## The nature of interactionist explanation

According to Herbert Blumer (1969), three key principles underpin most kinds of interactionist analysis. First, humans act towards things – other people, categories of person, objects, institutions, activities, situations – on the basis of *meanings*. Few, if any, human actions are meaningless, even though they may sometimes appear so to the observer. The difficulty lies in trying to understand what they mean to the person concerned. Thus, the key to understanding why some people react less than positively to health education about, say, tooth decay or to understanding why some people may react badly to a stay in hospital, is to try to see the situation from their point of view.

Second, meanings are not pre-given but derive from past experience and processes of social interaction. Objects and events do not have fixed meanings. Instead, they are *made to mean* various things by the interactions people have with one another. For example, to some people a Filofax may be a status symbol, to others it may simply be a useful way of keeping track of information, and to yet others it may be a sign of gross pretentiousness. Similarly in the field of health care, a doctor's refusal to write a prescription may be interpreted by one person as a quite reasonable action given the over-prescribing that currently takes place, but by another as a sign of indifference, or perhaps even incompetence.

Third, meanings shift and change in the light of new experience. As a result, people's relationships to events, situations, and one another may also be modified. Thus, men with ear-rings may be variously perceived as cool, trendy, manly, effeminate, or simply old-fashioned depending on the viewer and the circumstances in which the judgement is made. Similarly the social meanings associated with tobacco use have shifted dramatically over time. In the 1930s and 1940s, for example, it was sophisticated to smoke, whereas in the 1980s it is generally considered unhealthy and anti-social to do so. Indeed, in Britain today the tobacco industry has become so concerned about this situation that it has invested large sums of money in media campaigns promoting the supposed rights of smokers.

Taken together, these basic premises make up the key elements of interactionist analysis. They suggest that the social world is constructed out of the encounters people have with one another. Women and men actively construct self-understandings, understandings of others, and understandings of events and situations, out of their social experience. The key to explaining human action, therefore, lies in an appreciation of these varied perceptions and meanings.

These ideas raise important questions about the research methods interactionist sociologists might use in their inquiries into health issues. In contrast to social-positivists, for whom structured interviews and questionnaires may be appropriate research techniques, interactionists tend to favour more informal kinds of data collection. These include semi-structured and open-ended interviews as well as participant observation. These methods enable researchers to get closer to the meanings that underpin human action and allow an appreciation of respondents' points of view.

## Activities

Working in groups of three of four, choose one of the following health issues and design a study to discover some of the meanings that underlie the actions described. Assume that you can collect data from only three or four people. Remember to select research methods that will allow you to remain true to the spirit of interactionism. Present your study to other members of your group and seek their help in refining it.

- a study of people with tooth decay who refuse to go to the dentist
- a study of lunchtime drinking amongst university lecturers
- a study of underage drinking
- a study of people with eye problems who refuse to visit the optician
- a study of overweight middle-aged businessmen

Before carrying out your study, you will need to discuss

1 who you will collect data from
2 how you will collect data
3 when you will collect data
4 the questions you will need to ask
5 the difficulties you might encounter in carrying out the study.

## Key concepts

A number of key ideas have been developed as a result of interactionist inquiry, and between them they establish a useful framework by which to analyse different social situations. In the space available here, only some of the better known of these concepts can be discussed.

## Interpretation

Central within interactionist thought is the idea that the meaning of human encounters is rarely given. Rather, it must be constructed by participants and observers through *interpretation*. In writing about this process, Herbert Blumer (1969) directs our attention towards the provisional and somewhat precarious nature of social existence, since what we may take to be true about a particular situation at one moment in time can easily be revised in the light of further evidence. People, objects, situations, and events are rarely what they seem; they are instead what they are *made* to seem.

An illustration of this process is shown graphically in a study by Julius Roth (1972) of the accident and emergency departments of six hospitals in the USA. Roth was interested in the way in which judgements of 'moral worth' came to be made of those admitted to hospital. On the basis of his observations, he was able to distinguish between those patients who were regarded as worthy of the full attention of the staff and those who were felt to be more undeserving. Among men, drunks, or those perceived to be drunk (the amount of alcohol actually consumed did not seem to matter in this respect), tended to be treated in this latter way. Once an individual's actions had been interpreted as evidence of drunkenness, their complaints were rarely treated seriously. As Roth puts it,

> Take for example, patients who are labelled as drunks. They are more consistently treated as undeserving than any other category of patient. They are frequently handled as if they were baggage when brought in by the police; those with lacerations are usually treated roughly by physicians; they are usually treated only for drunkenness and obvious surgical repair without being examined for other pathology; no one believes their stories; their statements are ridiculed; they are treated in an abusive or jocular manner; they are ignored for long periods of time. ... Emergency ward personnel frequently comment on how they hate to take care of drunks.
> (Roth 1972: 849)

Amongst women, on the other hand, persistent abdominal pain with a temperature provoked a similar response, particularly if the woman concerned was black, young, unmarried, and working class in speech and appearance. Symptoms such as these were generally interpreted as evidence of 'a dissolute sex life, unwanted pregnancy and perhaps venereal disease, illegal abortion, and consequent infection of the reproductive organs' (Roth 1972: 850). Thereafter, women with these symptoms tended to be treated as less deserving of prompt and considerate treatment.

Central among the factors influencing the responses of staff working in the emergency services are their interpretations of the actions and presenting symptoms of those with whom they come into contact. The strategies staff use by which to allocate individuals to 'worthy' and 'less worthy' categories rely heavily on stereotypes and prejudiced judgement. These processes of *typification* are not, however, restricted to those working in accident and emergency units, but inform the judgements of staff caring for people in a wide range of settings.

## The self

In 1900 Wilhelm Dilthey wrote 'It is only by comparing myself with others that I experience the individual in me' (cited in Connerton 1976: 105). In these few words, he captures one of the fundamental ideas in interactionist theory – the concept of self. People are unique in that through their interactions with others they come to develop a sense of self. According to Charles Cooley (1909: 121), we construct ideas about ourselves by observing the reflections in others' reactions towards us. Cooley coined the phrase the *looking-glass self* to describe this process of identity formation. Of particular importance in this respect are their interaction we have with *significant others* – those with whom we have close and lasting relationships. According to George Herbert Mead (1934), it is through our interactions with significant others that we learn to *role-take*, taking first the roles offered by those who are close to us, and later the roles offered by society at large.

Ideas like these influenced the work of anti-psychiatrists such as R.D. Laing and David Cooper who, in the 1960s, wrote extensively about conditions such as schizophrenia. Rejecting the dominant theories of the time, they suggested that the delusions and feelings of persecution that often result in the diagnosis of schizophrenia can best be understood as strategies which the person has developed to live in an otherwise unlivable situation. For Laing (1961), Laing, and Esterson (1964), and Cooper (1971), schizophrenia is not a disease, still less the consequence of clear-cut social causes, but a meaningful response to the contradictions and tensions of family life.

The case of Claire Church, who had spent five years in hospital by the time she met Laing, illustrates this argument. Diagnosed as paranoid schizophrenic and persecuted by the belief that other people were tormenting her, Claire had received electro-convulsive therapy on many occasions, but with little improvement in her condition. Laing's inquiries soon revealed, however, that in Claire's eyes anyway, she had never been allowed to lead her own life. During subsequent discussions with her mother, Laing discovered that there seemed to be some substance to this claim.

> Claire's mother has always been under the impression that she knows Claire's feelings very well, because they are so *very* alike. She pointed out that both had mothers who were 'businesswomen'. Neither saw much of their mothers. But both had mothers who 'did everything for them ...' The similarity between mother and daughter's family constellations as seen by the mother led her to think that she knew what her daughter's 'feelings' were better than Claire knew herself!
>
> (Laing and Esterson 1964: 79–80)

As a result, Mrs Church tended to reject her daughter's view of the world. Instead, she redefined Claire's feelings for her, as

97

and when the occasion arose. Under these circumstances, Claire's sense of self and the persecution she feels can be seen as reasonable responses to the predicament she has found herself in. Numerous other case studies of this kind can be found in Laing's writing.

## The definition of the situation

In any social setting in which communication takes place, a working consensus or *negotiated order* develops between the parties involved (Mead 1934). This allows interaction to occur without too much interruption. It also establishes a taken-for-grantedness about what is going on. Without this, we would have continually to ask ourselves and others what is happening – are we in a party or a lecture? Is this a situation in which we can talk intimately about our sexual fantasies or is it an interview for a job? Clearly communication would break down if we had to ask questions like these all the time.

The negotiated order within a social setting contributes to what William Thomas (1923) has called the *definition of the situation* – a set of assumptions about the nature of the circumstances in which the action is taking place. Often the definitions of the situation arises from consensus and mutual agreement between participants, as is the case when, say, visiting the dentist. On such occasions, those seeking treatment will usually open their mouths when asked to, in order to allow the dentist to inspect their teeth. Rarely are they likely to refuse because, by mutual consent, the situation has been defined as one in which it is natural that this should take place.

Sometimes, however, situations can be defined for us without our explicit agreement. This often happens in the health field when doctors and other health professionals may seek to impose their own definitions upon us. There is now a considerable literature which identifies the dissatisfaction many people experience when trying to communicate with doctors (Cartwright 1967; Gregory 1978). At least part of the problem here may stem from the fact that whereas the person visiting the doctor may want to talk in general terms about their ill-health, the doctor may be trying to fit what is being said into pre-given bio-medical categories.

In a recent study of doctors' talk, Patrick Byrne and Barrie Long (1976) report that over three-quarters of the sixty general practitioners they observed used either a 'gathering information' or an 'analysing and probing' style of interview. Doctors often switched from one of these styles to another throughout the consultation, but what both share in common is that they allow little room for patients' feelings once an initial complaint has been identified. One of the more graphic illustrations of this process can be seen in the following exchange recorded in Malcolm Coulthard and Margaret Ashby's study of doctor-patient interviews.

Doctor:   Have you ever had any serious illnesses in the past?
Patient:  No.
Doctor:   No rheumatic fever?
Patient:  No, doctor.
Doctor:   Pleurisy?
Patient:  No, doctor.
Doctor:   Pneumonia?
Patient:  No, doctor.

(Coulthard and Ashby 1976: 80)

Here, the doctor makes little attempt to enter into the patient's world or to see the situation from his or her point of view. Instead, an existing framework consisting of medically defined disease categories is superimposed on the experiences the patient has had. The patient's involvement in the process of diagnosis is limited to agreement or disagreement with each category offered.

## Social identities and labelling

Interactionist accounts are sometimes said to suggest that there is little or no stability in the social world. If self-understandings are so volatile, and situations can be re-defined so readily, is there anything of permanence in human existence? But to criticize in this way is to do violence to interactionist explanations. Obviously there are human qualities that remain relatively constant across situations – if they were not, human behaviour would display an alarming degree of inconsistency. These personal qualities make up what Erving Goffman (1959; 1963) has called *social identities*, and they are associated with routine ways of acting, or *scripts*.

---

## Activities

1  In order to examine some of the scripts that underpin the way you act, write down the sequence of events that usually takes place when you wake up on a weekday morning. What do you do first of all? What do you do next? What happens after this? Share your list with a friend. How does their early morning script differ from your own?
2  Repeat the exercise for a Saturday or Sunday morning. Is there a difference in the script you follow at the weekend?
3  Now discuss 'who wrote the script'? Where did it come from?

---

Social identities are often strengthened by the reactions of others towards us, as well as by the labels that may be given to the way in which we behave. These processes can be seen clearly in David Rosenhan's (1973) study of what happened when eight sane people gained secret admission to twelve US mental hospitals, complaining that they had been hearing empty, hollow voices. Without exception, all were admitted, and the majority were diagnosed as schizophrenic. Following admission, each pseudo-patient ceased simulating any symptoms of abnormality and kept detailed notes on their experience.

In his report, Rosenhan describes what he calls the 'stickiness' of the diagnostic labels given to the pseudo-patients. Thus while other patients were quick to detect the relative sanity of those admitted, physicians and nurses never did so. Indeed, in the eyes of health professionals, once a person had been identified as abnormal, the label was so powerful that their subsequent relatively ordinary behaviour was either overlooked or seriously misinterpreted. As a result, the note-taking that pseudo-patients undertook during their stay in hospital tended to be interpreted either as pathology or as evidence of memory problems. Similarly the behaviour of a pseudo-patient who was waiting outside the cafeteria half-an-hour before lunch because he had nothing else to do was felt by a passing psychiatrist to be clear evidence of 'oral-acquisitive syndrome'. The length of time pseudo-patients spent in hospital varied from seven to fifty-two days, with an average of nineteen days.

Rosenhan's study shows the ease with which people can be *stigmatized*, as 'spoiled identities' are conferred upon them (Goffman 1963). It also drew attention to the serious consequences of being labelled 'diseased', 'sick', 'insane', or 'ill'. Indeed, in Rosenhan's study there was clear evidence that once pseudo-patients had been diagnosed as mentally ill, the reactions of staff towards them took on quite bizarre qualities. For example, Rosenhan describes the following interchange between a doctor and a pseudo-patient after the latter asked when he would be allowed to walk in the hospital grounds.

(pseudo-patient) 'Pardon me, Dr X. Could you tell me when I am eligible for grounds privileges?' (physician) 'Good morning, Dave. How are you today?' (moves off without waiting for a response).

(Rosenhan 1973: 256)

On other occasions, staff were verbally and physically abusive to patients, using obscene language, for example, to rouse them in the morning. Once diagnosed, patients were also denied privacy, were made to undress publicly in front of others, and were denied access to their own possessions. All of these processes contributed to powerlessness and depersonalization, as the individual identities of pseudo-patients were stripped away.

## Mortification and degradation

Rosenhan is not the only researcher to identify these kinds of effects. Goffman's (1968) earlier work in a Washington mental hospital enabled him to examine some of the rituals to which patients are frequently subjected. These include public undressing and washing, the removal and listing of personal possessions for storage, and photographing and fingerprinting. All of these processes resulted in a *mortification* of the self, or a breaking down of the self-identity which the individual had when they first arrived in the institution.

Degradation ceremonies of this kind can have important consequences for identity formation. In particular, they may lead some people to internalize the labels given them, incorporating them into their identities. Thus, someone who has been labelled neurotic may begin to construct a neurotic identity in the light of this. Similarly another person who has been labelled dangerous may start to behave dangerously towards others. This kind of behaviour, which is a consequence of the reactions of others towards us, has been described by Edwin Lemert (1967) as *secondary deviation* to distinguish it from *primary deviation*, which is part of the natural diversity of human biological and social characteristics.

## Careers

Goffman's research in hospitals and other total institutions led him to identify two stages in what he described as the *career* of the mental patient. The first of these involved the breaking down of the old self via processes of mortification.

The second involved the reconstruction of a new self as the individuals adjusted to life in the mental hospital. Some of the modes of adjustment identified by Goffman include *retreatism* in which individuals withdraw from the world, *conversion* in which individuals accept the label offered them, *colonization* whereby individuals swiftly incorporate themselves into the life of the institution, and *playing it cool* whereby individuals adjust to their surroundings in such a way that they are likely to maximize the chance of an early discharge.

Howard Becker (1963; 1964) has also used the concept of career to identify the different stages people can pass through in assuming a social identity. While his own work looked closely at 'deviant' forms of behaviour such as marijuana use, similar ideas, as we shall see, can be applied to the study of *health careers*.

Having identified some of the key concepts that underpin interactionist analyses of health and illness, in the remainder of this chapter we will look briefly at some recent examples of research carried out within this framework.

### Using heroin

It is all too easily forgotten in the midst of current moral outrage about heroin use that opiates (drugs like heroin derived from the opium poppy) have been used since at least 1500BC, that in Galen's time opium was believed to be a cure for 'vertigo, deafness, epilepsy, dimness of sight, loss of voice, asthma, coughs of all kinds, spitting of blood, tightness of breath, colic' (Scott 1969: 111), that Britain went to war with China on more than one occasion in the nineteenth century to protect its rights to trade in opium (Johnson 1975), and that as late as 1889, morphine was being heralded as an effective treatment for all manner of complaints, from lumbago to alcoholism (Ray 1978). In the USA elixirs and patent medicines liberally laced with opiates – with names such as Mrs Winslow's Soothing Syrup, the Infant's Friend, Ayer's Cherry Pectoral, and Godfrey's Cordial – were widely available from general stores throughout much of the last century (Conrad and Schneider 1980).

This century has, however, seen a range of very different responses to opiate use – and heroin in particular has been widely portrayed as a major social evil. In the space available here, we cannot discuss the complex political factors that led to the medicalization and criminalization of heroin use, but we can discuss findings from two studies conducted within a broadly interactionist framework which raise important questions about the inevitability of dependency and 'addiction'.

Since the 1940s Alfred Lindesmith and his colleagues have been examining the factors that result in some opiate users' becoming dependent on the drugs they use and others not. The starting-point for this research was the observation that while many people consume opiates, only a few come to rely on them physically or psychologically. For example, many of those who are prescribed diamorphine in hospital as a relief for serious pain experience little distress when the drug is subsequently withdrawn. But how would they react if they knew that diamorphine is in fact the same thing as heroin?

This question was the starting-point for Lindesmith's (1947; 1968) research. From his interviews with those who had used opiates, he developed the idea that opiate dependency occurs only when the individual knows what he or she is taking. This notion had to be revised, however, when one of the first people interviewed, a doctor, stated that he had taken morphine for several weeks, was well aware of the fact, but had not become dependent. Lindesmith revised his initial hypothesis to suggest that withdrawal distress as well as the knowledge that opiates are being used is essential for dependency. However, this hypothesis too had to be modified when he found a number of people who experienced distress when they discontinued opiate use, but who did not revert to drug-taking to alleviate it. What seemed to matter, therefore, was not whether or not a person experienced withdrawal distress, but how the individual dealt with these feelings.

Eventually Lindesmith was forced to conclude that a number of conditions are necessary for dependency to occur. First, there must be bodily and psychological changes after the drug is removed. Second, these bodily and/or psychological changes must be interpreted as withdrawal distress. Third, opiates have to be used to alleviate this distress. Dependency on a drug such as heroin is therefore by no means inevitable, but is influenced by how individuals perceive the relationship between themselves and their drug use.

While Lindesmith's work is important in highlighting the key role played by *interpretation* in the process of becoming dependent, research by Geoffrey Pearson, Mark Gilman, and Shirley McIver is significant in pointing out the different levels of involvement that make up a heroin user's *career*. Following their interviews with sixty-seven users and ex-users in the north of England, they identify five different phases of drug involvement:

1 *Non-use*: During this phase, the person does not use heoin at all.
2 *Experimentation*: During this phase, the person will be offered heroin, usually within the context of a friendship network, and will use it.
3 *Occasional use*: During this phase, heroin may be used occasionally as and when the opportunity arises; the person may not use the drug at all for prolonged periods of time.
4 *Transitional use*: During this 'grey area', the person uses heroin regularly but may or may not feel dependent upon it.
5 *Addictive use*: During this phase the person uses heroin regularly and becomes dependent on it.

It is important to realize though that progression from one phase to another is by no means inevitable. As Pearson and his colleagues put it:

Some people do slide rapidly into habitual use and addiction, following the pattern of progressive decline and escalating drug consumption which characterises the dominant stereotypical image of the heroin addict. But other people can, and do, arrest their involvement at different points in this hierarchy of statuses, so that some people discontinue their heroin use after a brief flirtation with the drug, whereas others maintain stable patterns of occasional use over long periods of time.

(Pearson *et al.* 1985: 23)

## Having a migraine

Interactionist ideas have been used to analyse a wide range of health issues, and for our next example we will look at a phenomenon which affects hundreds of thousands of people in Europe and North America – migraine. In an insider's account of the condition, Sally Macintyre and David Oldman identify some of the different phases they passed through in their careers as migraine sufferers.

The first phase in Macintyre's migraine career took place when she was 12. At the time, it was a distinctly anomic experience since she found herself unable to name, predict, or account for the symptoms she felt. Only after several more attacks, and at the age of 17, was she able to identify the nature of the condition. She was helped in this process (phase two of the career) by being admitted to hospital for medical investigations. Once doctors had ruled out the possibility of a brain tumour, epilepsy, or another central nervous system disorder, she was informed that she had migraine. Thereafter she entered phase three of her migraine career. Throughout this, she came to understand herself as 'a basically normal person who periodically experienced transitory physical disturbances' (Macintyre and Oldman 1984: 272).

On arrival at university, Macintyre was encouraged to reinterpret her predicament when she was treated by a doctor who felt that migraine was typical of over-conscientious, neurotic, and intelligent women, role conflicts, and stressful life events. Far from being the passive host of disease, she was

106

now encouraged to see herself in phase four of her migraine career as the active producer of the condition she sought to avoid. Phase five began when, at another university, the doctor treating her there felt that the migraine was the consequence of deep-seated personality conflicts and wanted her to undergo psychoanalysis. Only after meeting another general practitioner through a friend did she enter the sixth phase, in which the main emphasis became that of prevention. Now at phase seven, she considers herself an 'expert' patient, knowing what she wants and using doctors as a resource to supply her with the drugs needed.

Oldman's experience was very different. His mother had experienced frequent migraine attacks in her own childhood and was therefore able to *normalize* those of her son. Bed, a dark room, a hot water bottle, and Lucozade were administered each time an attack took place. Phase one of Oldman's career was therefore considerably less anomic than that of Macintyre. In phase two, the relationship between the onset of migraine and precipitating events became clearer: the aftermath of school examinations and rugby matches proved particularly powerful triggers of attacks. Phase three in Oldman's career can be characterized by efforts to avoid (so far as is possible) the factors that precipitate attacks, and to use medication to control them when they do occur. Phase four has involved him 'topping up' the drugs prescribed with others borrowed from friends and relatives.

While both of these careers differ, they share certain features in common. Both involved encounters with the medical profession, and both were associated with efforts to modify the therapy prescribed. Moreover, both resulted in strategies by which Macintyre and Oldman were able to normalize their conditions, and thereby lead relatively unaffected lives.

## Becoming a leper

As a final example of interactionist sociology in action, we will look briefly at Nancy Waxler's (1981) study of the

107

processes by which people become lepers. The starting-point for this work was her observation that there are wide variations in the manner in which different societies respond to leprosy. In some countries such as Ethiopia, India, and Sri Lanka lepers are feared, shunned, and treated as social outcasts. In other such as Nigeria, Tanzania, and the USA, lepers are treated far more benevolently. Waxler's interest lay in analysing the social origins and the social consequences of these different patterns of response.

Leprosy is a condition which has a known bacterial cause, an effective treatment, and a predictable outcome. Therapy arrests the progression of the disease and renders the person non-infectious. In contrast to sterotypes of leprosy, which conjure up images of severe physical deformity, the most common symptoms include raised eczema-like patches, skin ulcers that will not heal, and loss of sensation in the skin. Only after many years of non-treatment do people with leprosy resemble popular stereotypes of the condition. Given this information, we might expect the typical career of someone with leprosy to conform to the following pattern: an initial stage with mild symptoms that are probably un-recognizable to the layperson, medical diagnosis, treatment with appropriate forms of chemotherapy, the disappearance of symptoms, and the arrest of the disease.

Waxler's study shows, however, that rarely is this ideal sequence of events followed. Partly as a consequence of societal reaction and partly as a result of the way in which people with leprosy construct their identities in response to dominant stereotypes of the disease, several possible outcomes seem possible. All of this suggests that in the twentieth century, if not before, people learn to become lepers. As Waxler puts it,

A society's expectations for lepers, its beliefs about them, have a significant influence on their experiences as sick people. If we examine what a particular patient does when he discovers he has leprosy, we find that his response to leprosy is consistent with society's expectations for lepers. In fact, he learns to be a leper, the kind of leper his family and neighbours, even his doctors, expect him to be.

(Waxler 1981: 181)

Thus in Ethiopia it is relatively likely that the person will be rejected by close members of their household and be encouraged to leave home. Similarly it is likely that they will cease to have sexual relationships and, amongst those who are married, separation and divorce is high (Giel and Van Luijk 1970). In the USA, on the other hand, the dominant pattern of response is quite different. While a few may accept dominant definitions of the disease and withdraw from society, many respond wholeheartedly to their diagnosis by fighting back in what Waxler describes as a peculiarly 'American' way.

They become professional educators, acting as representatives of all lepers in an attempt to change the public's view of the disease. They give talks at Rotary clubs, organize seminars, speak about leprosy on the radio, conduct tours of the leprosy hospital. ... The content of their educational attempts is a new set of beliefs about leprosy, beliefs that are designed to replace the 'old' ideas that justified stigma.

(Waxler 1981: 182)

Given these differences, it would seem that becoming a leper is a process affected by personal experience, dominant ideas about the disease and moral definitions of what it means to have leprosy. Waxler's study is important not only because it demonstrates how people can construct very different self-understandings in relation to the same biological condition, but also because it identifies the role of broader societal factors in shaping the form that these take. In the next chapter, we shall examine some of these wider influences in more detail.

## Activities

1 In order to consolidate your understanding of the issues discussed in this chapter, make notes on the following key concepts: interpretation, the self, the definition of the situation, negotiated order, stigma, mortification, degradation ceremony, labelling, career.

2 Choose an illness which you or someone close to you has had in the last five years. With a partner, identify which of the concepts in the above list are helpful in making sense of the following stages of the experience:

- the stage when it was first suspected that something might be wrong
- the process of diagnosis
- the point at which the nature of the illness became clear
- the events that then followed.

## Further reading

A considerable amount of research into health and illness has been carried out within an interactionist perspective. Although written some time ago, Goffman's (1968) study of asylums is still well worth reading. Rosenhan's (1973) study entitled 'On being sane in insane places' has been widely reprinted, and can be found in a collection of articles edited by Albrecht and Higgins (1979), alongside Roth's paper on the moral evaluation of patients in accident and emergency units.

The concept of career has been widely used in interactionist accounts, and a classic collection of papers edited by Spitzer and Denzin (1968) applies the concept to the study of mental illness. Conrad and Schneider (1980) provide a compelling analysis of the tendency for deviance to have become medicalized throughout the twentieth century. A number of studies of doctor–patient interaction can be found in Wadsworth and Robinson (1976), and a book by Mishler et al. (1981) reports on a wide range of recent studies carried out within an interactionist perspective.

Chapter 4 in Parker et al. (1988) provides an insider view of drug careers involving the use of heroin, and a book by Welbourne and Purgold (1984) offers a useful perspective on what it means to become anorexic. Denzin's (1987) recent book on alcohol dependency offers a fascinating analysis of some of the social meanings of alcohol use and moves well beyond the view that alcoholism is a physical or psychological addiction.

# 6

## Structuralist explanations

So far we have discussed a variety of ways in which health, disease, and illness can be explained. Some of these have emphasized the biological determinants of health while others have addressed a range of more social considerations. What all of these explanations lack, however, is a systematic analysis of two things: *power* and the *broader social context* in which health, disease, and illness are defined.

Ill-health is not randomly distributed across the population (see chapter 2). Instead, for any chosen measure, some groups are systematically healthier than others. These inequalities raise important questions about the social determinants of health. In particular, they suggest that there are influences beyond individuals and groups which determine patterns of health, disease, and illness.

Reference has also been made to the power of some groups to define for themselves, and for others, what health is. In the previous chapter, for example, we discussed some of the ways in which psychiatrists and doctors are likely to label particular actions as signs of mental illness. We also examined some of the difficulties facing those who try to challenge these definitions. But there are other situations too in which questions of power become paramount. These include those in which people may be systematically denied access to the resources by which they can maintain their own health and that of others.

Both of these factors have encouraged some sociologists to develop structuralist explanations of health. These emphasize the relationship between health and the structure of society as a whole. Two rather different kinds of structuralist explanation will be examined: those developed by *Marxist* sociologists, which emphasize the role that capitalism plays in creating health inequalities, and those developed by *feminist* sociologists, which emphasize the corresponding effects due to patriarchy, or male power.

## Capitalism and health

As part of Karl Marx's interest in the origins and consequences of different economic systems, he compared the capitalist economies of Britain and other European countries with other social arrangements, such as those in agrarian and feudal societies. He was particularly interested in three things: *economic systems*, the relationships or *social relations* to which they give rise, and the forms of *subjectivity* or consciousness that are associated with them. In the twentieth century neo-Marxist writers such as Louis Althusser and Nicos Poulantzas have developed these ideas further in their analyses of modern capitalist societies.

Central within Marxist analysis is the idea that the economy is a powerful determinant of social, political, and cultural life. Thus feudalism as an economic system gave rise to particular ways of living, particular roles and responsibilities, and particular forms of consciousness. Similarly capitalism established certain relationships between people which in turn gave rise to particular ways of seeing the world and acting within it. Marxist sociologists differ from one another, however, in

113

the extent to which they believe that the economy is all important in determining social existence. Some of them argue that the economy exerts a powerful influence over these aspects of society whereas others suggest that social institutions and social groups have some freedom or *relative autonomy* when it comes to determining how social life takes place. What all Marxist sociologists share, however, is an interest in historical analysis. Thus in making sense of modern capitalist economies and their consequences, it is essential to look at the past.

## Early capitalism

According to Bryan Turner, early capitalist societies such as nineteenth-century Britain, Germany, or France, have five key characteristics:

> the private ownership and control of the means of production, the organization of economic activity for the pursuit of profit, the existence of a market that regulates such activity, the social appropriation of economic profits by the personal owners of capital, and the provision of labour power by workers.
>
> (Turner 1987: 176)

In such societies, there is a major social division between those who own the means of production, and whose interests lie in the maximization of profit, and those who have only their labour to sell. Marx called these two groups the capitalist class (or bourgeoisie) and the working class (or proletariat) respectively.

Given that the main interest of the capitalist class lies in maximizing profits, in early capitalist societies there are likely to be high levels of industrial accidents and high levels of environmental pollution. For the situation to be otherwise, there would have to be an unacceptable reduction in profit. Social conditions like these prevailed throughout much of the last century. As Frederick Engels put it in 1844:

The manner in which the great multitude of the poor is treated by society today is revolting. They are drawn into large cities where they breathe a poorer atmosphere than in the country ... they are deprived of all means of cleanliness. ... They are given damp dwellings, cellar dens that are not waterproof from below. ... They are supplied bad, tattered or rotten clothing, adulterated or indigestible food. [They] are worked every day to the point of complete exhaustion of their mental and physical energies. ... How is it possible, under such conditions, for [them] to be healthy and long lived?

(in Black *et al.* 1984: 61)

## Modern capitalism

Modern capitalist economies, such as the USA, West Germany, or Britain today, differ from early ones in a number of significant respects. While the basic class division between capitalists and working class remains, the picture is complicated by a growing separation between the ownership and the control of capital. This gives rise to a new social grouping – the *new middle class* – whose role it is to manage, control, and service production; included within the new middle class are technicians, managers, teachers, and health care workers.

Additionally in modern capitalist societies, the *state* assumes increasing responsibility for health, education, and welfare of the workforce as a result of political alliances between the capitalist class and 'democratically' elected representatives. As Turner puts it:

Although the requirement for continuous and regular production with a submissive and healthy workforce is a basic feature of capitalist production, the capitalist does not want to bear the burden of financing the health, education and welfare of the workforce. Given the requirement for profit, the capitalist seeks to avoid these social costs. Therefore in capitalism, the state has a role to play in regulating, educating and providing services for the workforce.

(Turner 1987: 172)

115

## Capitalism and the causes of ill-health

In their analysis of the economic and political determinants of health, Doyal and Pennell (1979) identify some of the ways in which capitalism can be implicated directly or indirectly as a cause of illness and disease. Adverse physical effects include occupational hazards such as poisonous dusts and fumes, unsafe working procedures, dangerous machinery, and environmental and atmospheric pollution arising from capitalists' desire to maximize profits at the expense of making adequate provision for the re-processing of waste products.

Threats to physical health may also be posed by particular patterns of consumption. Here Doyal and Pennell single out smoking and the increased consumption of processed foods low in nutritional value. Every year, millions of pounds is spent promoting the sale of products such as these. The state's role with respect to intervention in these markets is at best ambivalent – being restricted to 'moral exhortation' and 're-education' to persuade people to adopt healthier patterns of consumption, rather than intervention at the level of the producer.

---

### Activities

Capitalism is an economic system organized on the basis of production for profit.
1 Working in small groups, find out about the following kinds of business using the library, after first adding two or three local industries to the list.
2 Identify the threats to physical health that could arise from the owners of each business trying to maximize their profits. Distinguish between those threats affecting employees and those affecting people living nearby.
   ● a small business dealing in scrap metal
   ● a medium-sized transport business with a fleet of lorries
   ● a large private hospital

- a sports or leisure centre.

---

Doyal and Pennell also discuss the threats to mental health that capitalism creates through alienation: the misery and unfulfilment that arises when work is external to the individual and his or her interests. In capitalist societies, few employees have control over the circumstances in which they work, the pace at which production takes place, or what is done with the goods or services they produce. The discontent that results from this kind of production can be seen in high absenteeism and sickness rates as well as in general apathy and discontent. Capitalist production has other consequences too in that its instability causes periodic unemployment, with attendant threats to psychological well-being. Furthermore, capitalism requires women to undertake a dual role: as providers of domestic labour and as employees in times of economic need. This creates a special set of stresses for them which are reflected in accidents and injuries at home as well as in high rates of depression and anxiety.

Finally, Doyal and Pennell identify some of the international consequences of capitalism for health and well-being. Some of these can be traced back to colonialist expansion when countries such as Britain, Germany, France and Spain occupied vast areas of the globe in the pursuit of cheap raw materials and cheap sources of labour. As a result, infectious diseases of all kinds were transported around the world, often with catastrophic consequences. For example, measles and smallpox were taken to the Americas by Spanish imperialists, and the slave trade introduced yellow fever and leprosy to the same continent a hundred years later.

Other international effects can be attributed to malnutrition caused by colonialist desires to transform indigenous agricultural arrangements to the production of cash crops. In African and Caribbean countries, the most fertile land was taken by plantation owners to grow single crops such as sugar, tea, and coffee. This had serious consequences for the health of local people who had hitherto relied on this land to provide them with a balanced diet.

In the twentieth century the growth of capitalism in Europe and North America has contributed to the under-development of many Third World countries. Work conditions which would be unthinkable in the First World have been imposed on people with little power to resist, with their attendant health consequences. Additionally dangerous industrial manufacturing processes have been located in some Third World countries where there are less stringent environmental and employment controls. The latter part of the twentieth century has also seen an increase in *iatrogenic* (medically induced) illness in under-developed countries, with western pharmaceutical companies testing new drugs on the local population and continuing to sell those that have been withdrawn from home markets on safety grounds (Melrose 1982).

## Capitalism and health care

In capitalist societies, private, individual, and voluntary systems of health care exist alongside those provided by the state. In countries such as Germany and Austria, social insurance was introduced in the late nineteenth century. In Britain, a similar set of arrangements was implemented in 1911 and consolidated in 1948 with the setting up of the National Health Service. The USA was slower to develop a universal system of state provision, with Medicare and Medicaid programmes being introduced only in the mid-1960s.

According to Vicente Navarro (1976), the capitalist state's involvement in health care brings about three things: it reproduces the class structure, it reproduces individualist ideology, and it reproduces alienation. The first of these outcomes is realized via the hierarchies among health workers. In modern capitalist societies, doctors are usually middle-class men, whereas nurses and health auxiliaries are usually lower middle-class or working-class women. Thus the structure of the bio-medical hierarchy reproduces existing class and gender divisions.

With respect to ideology, state involvement in health care sustains ideas and practices which suggest that the causes of ill-health reside within individuals and their behaviour. Bio-medicine as it is practised in modern capitalist economies rarely focuses on the economic and political factors responsible for illness and disease.

Finally, state involvement in health care reproduces alienation. One of the roots of alienation lies in divisions between those who govern and those who are governed, those who administer and those who are administered, and those who are experts and those who are the recipients of 'expertise'. In modern capitalist economies, doctors and other health professionals are the governors and experts. As a result, their clients may feel isolated from the means by which they might recover their health and well-being.

According to Navarro, two kinds of mechanisms bring about the effects described – positive and negative selection mechanisms. The former directly promote capitalism, the latter deal with events that threaten capitalism's continued existence.

Positive selection mechanisms

Positive selection mechanisms include what Claus Offe (1975) has called *allocative* intervention policies such as the requirement on doctors to record the existence and development of epidemic disease that might otherwise threaten production. Other policies of this kind can be seen in the minimal legal framework that governs health and safety at work. Positive selection mechanisms also include *productive* intervention policies such as state involvement in medical education, in the management of hospitals and medical research, and in the production of drugs and medical equipment.

## Negative selection mechanisms

There are four kinds of negative selection mechanism. *Structural* mechanisms include the notable absence of legislation to protect workers against many of the hazards of industrial production. *Ideological* mechanisms, on the other hand, include the forces that encourage us to understand illness in individualistic rather than social terms (see p. 88). *Decision-making* mechanisms include the processes whereby selection and appointment to influential bodies such as Regional and District Health Authorities in Britain, and Health System Agencies in the USA are likely to favour those from upper- and upper-middle-class backgrounds. Finally, *repressive-coercion* mechanisms are those that through direct force defuse threats to capitalist interests. In Britain they may include central government efforts to privatize sections of the health service such as cleaning and catering, and perhaps in time even the provision of health care itself.

### Capitalism and the power of medicine

Central in any Marxist analysis of health and health care is the concept of power, and nowhere is this more relevant then in making sense of the medical profession and its practices. Until recently, much of the sociological literature on this topic has been written from either a functionalist or a Weberian perspective. Within the former tradition, doctors have the important task of confirming individuals in the *sick role* – a socially sanctioned set of behaviours to which we are expected to conform when we are sick (Parsons 1951).

Within a Weberian tradition, sociologists such as Eliot Freidson (1970) have examined the rational-legal basis of doctors' authority. Rejecting the idea that physicians are altruists who work simply to serve the community, Freidson discusses how, in the twentieth century, doctors have secured a monopoly over health care. He concludes that they have achieved this goal by political means.

The foundation of medicine's control over its work is thus clearly political in character. ... The occupation itself has formal representatives, organisational or individual, which attempt to direct the efforts of the state towards policies desired by the occupational group. ... Thus it is by the interaction between formal agents or agencies of the occupation and officials of the state that the occupation's control over its work is established and shaped.

(Freidson 1988: 23)

The power of the medical profession therefore resides in its legal rights to office granted by the state, not in the knowledge or expertise of its members. As a result of the political alliances into which they have entered, doctors have now gained a degree of occupational autonomy shared by few other professions.

In contrast to functionalists and Weberians, Marxist sociologists have examined the relationship between the economy and medical power. In a critique of Freidson's work, John McKinley (1977) suggests that professional medicine is becoming increasingly reorganized so as to contribute to the maximization of profit. While his analysis was developed from research in the USA, many of the points he makes have increasing relevance to Britain in the late 1980s. Thus the interests of capital are served by profits from the sale of drugs and medical supplies, private health care insurance and treatment in private hospitals and clinics. According to McKinley, the professional socialization of doctors encourages them to recommend the most profitable treatments and therapies, and to focus their attention on cure rather than prevention. The power invested in doctors therefore derives from the role they play in helping to sustain and reproduce capitalist social relations.

We saw earlier that modern bio-medicine has an ideological role to play in capitalist societies by focusing attention on personal attributes and life-styles rather than on the broader social and economic determinants of ill-health (see

p. 88). It is within this context that the relative autonomy of doctors may best be understood. As paid employees of the state, or as individuals whose livelihood is directly or indirectly supported by the state regulation of welfare, doctors occupy an ambiguous location within the class structure, being neither capitalists, nor in a strict sense workers. Instead, they are allowed limited economic and political autonomy so long as they act in ways that coincide with the interests of capital.

## Patriarchy and health

So far we have discussed structuralist explanations which emphasize capitalism and class as major factors determining health. Recently feminist sociologists have developed a different kind of structuralist explanation which identifies the ways in which *patriarchy*, or male power, affects women's health experience.

According to Ann Popkin (1979: 199), patriarchy is 'the institutional all encompassing power that men have as a group over women, the systematic exclusion of women from power in society, and the systematic devaluation of all roles and traits that society has assigned to women'. Patriarchy structures perceptions and understandings of the world, and determines the ways in which women and men act. It establishes 'interdependence and solidarity among men that enable them to dominate women' (Hartmann 1981: 14), and is sustained by men's efforts to control women's labour power and restrict their sexuality. It also has important implications for women's experience of health, illness, and disease.

### Women and reproduction

For several thousand years, efforts have been made to define women's reproductive systems as intrinsically pathological. In Greek, Roman, and Egyptian medicine, for example, it was believed that the womb was an inherently unstable organ, prone to restive movement around the body. Its movement upwards towards the liver and heart was believed to be the cause of seizures, fits, convulsions, and hysteria. The womb was also believed to be intimately tied to women's emotional state, weakening their rationality and increasing their passion. The patriarchal (and heterosexist) basis of ideas like these is clearly shown by Galen's belief that hysteria did not occur in women who were 'fertile and receptive and eager to the advances of their husbands', but only in those whose 'retained uterine secretions caused bad blood, irritation of the nerves, and finally paroxysms' (Open University 1985b: 85).

Ancient Hebrew mythology was no less misogynist. Thus the book of Genesis presents childbirth as an inherently dangerous, painful, and terrifying experience – the supposedly just recompense for Eve having persuaded Adam to eat from the Tree of Knowledge (Arms 1975).

> Unto the woman he said, 'I will greatly multiply thy sorrow and thy conception; in sorrow thou shalt bring forth children; and thy desire shall be to thy husband, and he shall rule over thee'.
>
> (Genesis 3: 16 Authorized Version)

Throughout the Middle Ages, the Christian church consolidated beliefs about the pathology of women's sexuality through its obsession with witchcraft (Daly 1979). In the *Malleus Maleficarum*, for example, a book of guidance on the identification of witches, the Dominican friars Heinrich Kramer and Jacob Sprenger conclude that 'All witchcraft comes from carnal lust, which is in women insatiable' (Summers 1971: 47).

Patriarchal ideology operates within modern bio-medical discourse and informs the common sense of health professionals and lay people alike. Thus a whole host of negative terms is often used to describe women's reproductive system, conjuring up an image of an intrinsically unstable set of arrangements. As Naomi Pfeffer puts it:

123

A woman can suffer from *irregular* menstrual cycles caused by hormonal *imbalances* which can lead to *hostile* cervical mucus and *irregular* shedding of the lining of her uterus which may eventually become *retroverted*. If she does ovulate, she may fail to conceive because of *blocked* fallopian tubes, or she may conceive an *ectopic* or *wrongly placed* pregnancy. Then she faces the danger of *spontaneous* or even *habitual* miscarriage due perhaps to a *blighted* ovum or even an *incompetent* cervix.

(Pfeffer 1985: 32)

A comparable vocabulary describing the vagaries of men's reproductive anatomy simply does not exist. Medical and biological textbooks frequently describe their reproductive systems as simpler and more efficient than women's: being, for example, 'efficient factories' for the production of 'plucky', 'independent', and 'self-motivated' sperm (Pfeffer 1985). It should therefore come as no surprise to find that whereas modern bio-medicine has constructed a medical speciality for women's reproductive system (gynaecology), there is no equivalent for men. Lest it be thought that these arrangements reflect simple biological differences, it should be remembered that understandings such as these are culturally specific, strongly contested, and amenable to change over time. In recent years, women working in Women's Health have done much to challenge these ideas and to develop more positive understandings of women's reproductive capacities.

## Women and childbirth

An extension of some of the processes discussed above can be seen in nineteenth- and twentieth-century efforts to medicalize and pathologize childbirth. According to Ann Oakley, childbirth is both a biological and a cultural event.

Childbirth stands uncomfortably at the junction of the two worlds of nature and culture. Like death and disease it is a biological event, but the defining feature of biological events in human life is their social character. The way people are born and die, their assignations with illness and death, cannot be explained and predicted purely on the basis of knowledge about the biological functioning of the human organism. Bodies function in a social world, and the parameters of this world supply an influence of their own.

(Oakley 1980: 7)

Traditionally women have always had a key role to play in the delivery of children, and few societies have been without midwives of one kind or another. The nineteenth and twentieth centuries, however, have seen the rise of male-dominated medical specialities such as obstetrics. At first sight, developments such as these might uncritically be seen as the natural consequence of modern bio-medicine's tendency to replace more traditional systems of health care. A closer examination of events, however, points to the existence of sustained conflict between doctors and midwives over who should be involved in childbirth. In the USA, for example, controversy raged throughout much of the nineteenth century, with (male) physicians insisting that the rigours of childbirth necessitated the surgical and medical interventions that only they could make (Ehrenreich and English 1973) Barker-Benfield (1976: 66) has interpreted this as part of a 'persistent, defensive attempt to control and shape women's procreative power'.

In Britain too, there has been much debate about the role that male-dominated bio-medicine has played in determining the way in which women give birth. Not only has the rise of obstetrics been accompanied by a shift away from home births, but also it has witnessed a profound medicalization of childbirth itself. In 1927, 85 per cent of all children were born at home, but by 1980 this proportion had fallen to just over 1 per cent (Open University 1985b). In 1953, 2.2 per cent of children were born by Caesarean section, but by 1984 this figure had risen to 10 per cent. In 1953, 3.7 per cent of children were delivered by forceps or vacuum extraction, but by 1984 this figure had risen to 15 per cent (MacFarlane and Mugford 1984).

125

A hospital birth nowadays often involves the administration of drugs to induce labour, the administration of more drugs for pain relief, the electronic monitoring of the woman's contractions, the electronic monitoring of the foetal heart rate, surgery to enlarge the vaginal opening – and all this occurs with the woman lying on her back propped up with pillows. Is it any wonder that, when constructed this way, childbirth is for many women a restrictive and uncomfortable experience (Oakley 1980; Boyd and Sellars 1982)? In making sense of this move towards greater medicalization, Oakley and other feminists emphasize the transfer of control from women to men. As a result, childbirth has 'lost its character as a taken-for-granted aspect of adult life' and has 'caused women to be massively alienated from their reproductive function' (Oakley 1979: 165).

## Women and mental illness

Reference was made earlier to patriarchy's power to define certain perceptions and actions as normal and others as abnormal. As a result, many of women's experiences come to be systematically devalued by men, or regarded as signs of irrational behaviour or evidence of mental instability. Nowhere can this be seen more clearly than in psychiatry where, as recently as 1972, a widely used textbook went so far as to recommend psychosurgery for a depressed woman 'who may owe her illness to her psychopathic husband who can not change and will not accept treatment' (cited in Showalter 1987: 210). As Susan Penfold and Gillian Walker put it:

The institution of psychiatry presents itself as healing, benign and compassionate while obscuring its function ... as a social regulator. Where women are concerned, most psychiatric theories and practices validate the male as prototype, legitimate women's second-class status as male property, validate dominant-subordinate relationships between men and women, re-inforce the institution of

Motherhood as a sacred calling, urge women to view their identity in terms of their success as wife, mother and sexual companion. ... Thus psychiatry is a very powerful force towards preserving a situation which works for the material gain of men.

(Penfold and Walker 1984: 244)

Under the psychiatric gaze (see p. 59), women often constructed as deficient, emotionally unstable, or at the beck and call of their hormones. As a result, they are more likely than men to be prescribed psychotropic drugs, and to be blamed for the conditions they seek help for. This can be most clearly seen in medical responses to hysteria.

Contrary to popular belief, hysteria rarely manifests itself in the form of fits and screaming. More often, it appears as a collection of vague and diffuse symptoms of unknown origin – headaches, fainting spells, anxiety attacks, loss of vision or hearing, unexplained pains, and depression. Hysteria tends to be a chronic condition and is nearly always diagnosed in women. It is often taken as evidence of deep-seated unresolved anxieties or learned maladaptive behaviour. Women with hysteria have often been characterized as morally degenerate. As Maudsley, one of the founders of modern psychiatry, put it in 1895, 'nowhere [are there] more perfect examples of the subtlest deceit, the most ingenious lying, the most diabolic cunning, in the service of vicious impulses' (in Showalter 1987: 134).

Recently feminist sociologists have developed a far-reaching critique of ideas such as these. Arguing that what psychiatrists characterize as hysteria is little more than the dominant male stereotype of women's behaviour, writers such as Harriet Lerner have suggested that:

the diagnostic indicators of hysteria are very much in keeping with the media presentation of the female sex. ... I do believe there is a danger that the hysterical personality will be reduced to the description of a particular kind of feminine behaviour that has certain effects on a male observer.

(Lerner 1974: 159 and 162)

Evidence to support such a view comes from Karen Armitage's (1979) study of the behaviour of male doctors when presented with comparable medical complaints such as headaches, fatigue, and dizziness in women and in men. For each condition, male patients received a more thorough physical examination as efforts were made to identify an organic basis for the symptoms. Women on the other hand were more likely to receive a psychological diagnosis. Research such as this highlights the need for more sustained inquiry into the processes by which a predominantly male profession relates to its women clients.

## Women and the medical profession

Finally, we will examine the position of women in the medical hierarchy. In a recent study of women physicians, Judith Lorber (1984) documents the kinds of discrimination women are likely to come up against in the medical profession. In the USA women constitute less than a quarter of doctors overall, and Lorber identifies a number of mechanisms which ensure that women remain under-represented at the higher levels within the medical hierarchy and in certain medical specialities.

These include the judgements and actions of gatekeepers and sponsors within the profession which create a series of double binds for women in medicine. She cites the often-held view that 'if [women] are married, they are considered committed to their family rather than their career [but] if they are unmarried they are considered unreliable or dangerous protegées and colleagues because of the assumption that a sexual relationship is their prime priority'. Likewise, she argues that 'nurturant, emotional and supportive women are tracked into lower prestige work and not considered leadership material, but aggressive women are also heavily penalized

128

because of the implied threat to men's dominant position' (Lorber 1984: 11).

Lorber points to a number of processes which make it difficult for women to gain upward mobility within the profession. These include the 'sorting and tracking' that takes place in medical school whereby women are encouraged not to follow their own career choices but those deemed appropriate for them by men, the relative absence of women role models and women sponsors within the profession, and the persistence of overt discrimination against women by men. Additionally the attitudes of male spouses who may try to evade their own responsibilities in respect of child-care make it difficult for many women to progress within medicine.

Taken together, the mechanisms she describes provide ample evidence of the impact of patriarchal ideologies on a wide range of medical practices. The structure of the profession as well as broader societal determinants mean that in medicine as in other health care employment, the opportunities open to women and men are far from equal.

---

*Further reading*

*For those interested in neo-Marxist analyses of health, pp. 27–30 in Jones and Moon (1987) and pp. 22–7 of Doyal and Pennell (1979) provide a succinct overview of the key issues. Chapter 3 of Doyal and Pennell (1979) offers an informative, although largely descriptive, account of the health consequences of colonialism. The relationship between multinational drug companies and the Third World is well discussed in Melrose (1982).*

*Recent books by Griffith et al. (1987) and Collier (1989) analyse the role that capitalism has played in structuring medical priorities and medical practices. They both contain important chapters on the role of drug companies and the nature of medical professionalism. Similar ideas can be found in Watkins (1987) who gives a readable account of the politics of medicine in Britain today.*

*There is no shortage of material on the effects of patriarchy on women's experience of health. Homans (1986) has edited a collection of essays examining reproduction from a variety of feminist perspectives. Showalter (1987) and Penfold and Walker (1984) have written compelling accounts of women's experience of psychiatry. Chapters 7, 8, and 9 in Book 2* (Medical Knowledge: Doubt and Certainty) *of the Open University (1985b) course* Health and Disease (U205) *provide an excellent analysis of theories about hysteria.*

---

# 7

## Perspectives on health policy

So far, we have examined some of the different ways in which health can be defined, measured, and explained. In so doing, we have had to recognize that there is not one thing called 'health', neither is there only one way of measuring or explaining it. Instead, what counts as an appropriate definition, a suitable measurement, or an adequate explanation depends on the perspective adopted. Bio-medical positivists, social-positivists, interactionists, and structuralists all have their own views about these matters, as do professionals and lay people alike. For the sociologist, the most important thing is to be clear about the stance that is being taken – only then can one's own position and that of others be subjected to critical evaluation.

In this chapter we shall move away from these considerations to examine some of the health policy implications of the issues so far discussed. Before we do this, however, a word of caution. In no sense should what follows be seen as a comprehensive review of health policy and practice: to

131

undertake this would require a separate book. The objective here is more limited: an examination of some of the competing perspectives that can help in explaining existing patterns of health care provision. The emphasis will be on British experience, but many of the concepts apply to other settings.

## The problem of accounts

When I was at school, history meant remembering the names of 'famous' people (usually men) and the dates on which 'important' things happened. We used to have weekly tests, when our ability to recall these names and events would be assessed, and these were usually preceded by frantic attempts to rote learn the necessary information. This way of teaching about the past can still be encountered in some schools today, and it informs the accounts of health policy that can be found in many standard textbooks. It is not, however, the approach that will be adopted here.

This is not to say that people and dates are not important when it comes to understanding health policy – they are – but it is to call for a deeper analysis, one which reveals the complex forces that influence policy matters. As sociologists, we must be critical of explanations which suggest that events 'naturally' follow one from another, and which imply that social change has its origins in the actions of individuals. Instead, we should recognize that this kind of 'story-telling' offers only *one* perspective on events and needs to be judged for its adequacy against other accounts.

## The development of modern health policy – a conventional account

We will begin by considering first of all a typical account of the development of modern British health policy – one which, like the history lessons referred to above, highlights significant dates, influential individuals, well-known committees, and important Acts of Parliament. It is taken largely from Christopher

Ham's (1985) recent study of British health policy. For ease of reference, it is presented in tabular form (Table 7).

Table 7 *The development of modern health policy in Britain*

| | |
|---|---|
| 1848 Public Health Act | – Aimed to limit the spread of water-bourne infectious diseases by providing adequate water supplies and sewerage systems |
| 1872 and 1875 Public Health Acts | – Established sanitary authorities to provide public health services and also led to the appointment of local medical officers of health |
| 1911 National Insurance Act | – Introduced sickness and unemployment benefit and free general practitioner care for those on low incomes |
| 1919 Davidson Committee | – Recommended the creation of an integrated system of hospital and primary medical care |
| 1929 Local Government Act | – Transferred control of workhouses and infirmaries to local authorities, and required local authorities to provide hospitals for mentally ill and mentally handicapped people |
| Second World War | – Wartime Emergency Medical Service merged public hospitals with voluntary hospitals |
| 1942 Beveridge Report | – Laid the foundations for the National Health Service (NHS). Health care to be free at the point of consumption and paid for by state-provided health insurance |
| 1950–60 | – Capital expenditure on the NHS low |
| 1962 Hospital Plan | – Recommended creation of district general hospitals to provide all but the most specialized services |
| 1960s and 1970s | – Growing gulf between services provided by hospitals and general practitioners |
| 1974 | – First reorganization of NHS to improve administrative efficiency and (continued) |

133

|            |   | to achieve greater co-ordination between services |
| 1982       | – | Second reorganization of NHS to streamline administrative efficiency |
| 1980s      | – | Increasing concern about the quality of service provided by the NHS; long waiting lists seemed to suggest that demand was outstripping supply |
| 1983 Griffiths Report | – | Recommended appointment of general managers at all levels in the health service |
| 1989 White Paper | – | Plans for further reorganization to increase health service accountability; encouragement of private medicine, selected hospitals to 'opt out', general practitioners to be provided with cash-limited budgets |

*Source*: based on Ham (1985)

## The development of modern health policy – some alternative accounts

Alternative accounts of modern health policy examine the complexities that lie behind the events described above. They focus on processes as diverse as the impact of political ideologies on the policy-making process; the outcome of particular alliances between individuals, organizations, and interest groups; the interplay between central government, local authorities, and the voluntary sector; the impact of the economy on decision-making; and the role of the medical profession in determining policy priorities. Here, we will examine four different theoretical frameworks that can be used to make sense of the events described – liberalism, pluralism, Marxism, and feminism. Our discussion of them will be limited to what they have to say about certain key events.

### Liberalism

An important distinction needs to be drawn between *liberalism* as a perspective on events and the views of the modern

Liberal party (or the Democrats for that matter). Liberalism, or market liberalism as it is sometimes called, is a political philosophy which suggests that societies operate best when organized on free market principles. According to this point of view, the state should not interfere in the market, but should leave the provision of goods and services to the forces of supply and demand. Likewise, it should provide health and welfare services only for those who are genuinely in need. To do any more than this is to sap the energies of those who can adequately provide for themselves, and to encourage too high a set of expectations about what the state can offer.

The origins of views like these can be traced back to Adam Smith, whose book, *Inquiry into the Nature and Causes of the Wealth of Nations*, was published in 1776 and John Stuart Mill, whose book, *Principles of Political Economy*, was published in 1848. After a period of unpopularity in the post-war years, market liberalism enjoyed a revival in the 1970s and 1980s, and has influenced the ideas of many Conservative politicians in Britain and Republicans in the USA. As a result, its principles have informed a wide range of social and economic policies in both of these countries, where modern market liberalism is often referred to as the politics of the New Right.

New Right perspectives on events leading to the setting up of the NHS and the welfare state emphasize the negative effects of state involvement of this kind. As Milton and Rose Friedman put it:

Most of the present welfare programmes should never have been enacted. If they had not been, many of the people now dependent on them would have become self-reliant individuals instead of wards of state. In the short run, that might have appeared cruel for some, leaving them no option to low-paying unattractive work. But in the long run, it would have been far more humane.

(Friedman and Friedman 1980: 119)

They also suggest that state intervention in health has generated unrealistic public expectations about what the state can provide, with demands for health care far outstripping the available resources. According to David Green (1987), the remedy to the present crisis within the Health Service lies in improving consumer choice. This can be achieved by encouraging a switch to private health insurance, by allowing hospitals and general practitioners to sell their services in an open market, and by giving the private sector a greater role in health care provision. This, he argues, will ensure that there are improvements in quality and efficiency.

## Pluralism

In contrast to liberal analyses, pluralist perspectives take a more positive view of state involvement in health care. For pluralists, society consists of a multitude of social groups, each with its own interests and priorities. In what are often called conventional pluralist accounts, the state is seen as a neutral arbiter between these groups and the policies they advocate. In neo-pluralist accounts, on the other hand, the state is afforded a more expansive role as a guide and mentor to those who may need its help.

Like liberals, pluralists accept the framework provided by capitalism, but they are more sceptical about the free market's ability to provide adequately for health care needs. Adopting a broadly social-positivist analysis, pluralists typically point to the profound health inequalities that existed in the nineteenth century – the heyday of the free market. These, they argue, were created by the imperfections of capitalism, and required intervention by the state if their worst effects were to be ameliorated.

In the years leading up to the 1911 National Insurance Act, pluralist perspectives were influential in persuading a variety of politicians that state intervention in health and welfare could have lasting benefits for those who were destitute, correcting moral defects, acting as a guardian for those who were unable to provide for themselves, and providing support to those in need (Clarke *et al.* 1987).

136

In the debates leading to the setting up of the NHS, similar ideas were expressed, with pluralists emphasizing the importance of altruism as an important rationale for state involvement in health care. In reflecting on these events some twenty years later, Richard Titmuss comments:

the ways in which society organizes and structures its social institutions can encourage or discourage the altruistic in [people]; such systems can foster integration or alienation; they can allow ... generosity towards strangers to spread among and between social groups and generations. This ... is an aspect of freedom in the twentieth century which, compared with the emphasis on consumer choice in material acquisitiveness, is insufficiently recognised.

(Titmuss 1970: 226)

Throughout the 1950s and 1960s neo-pluralists advocated the pursuit of a rational approach to health planning, and argued that specialists and professionals had an important part to play in the social administration of the emerging welfare state. Their task was socially to engineer the most desirable outcomes: full employment, social security, and an overall reduction in illness and disability. When crisis struck the NHS in the late 1970s, neo-pluralists were thrown into disarray. Their desire for balance and compromise in political decision-making was much at odds with the offensive of New Right politicians keen to dismantle post-1948 health care provision.

As a result, there has been some fragmentation amongst pluralists. On the one hand, there are those such as Peter Townsend (1984) who argue for enhanced social planning as a means of reducing health inequalities. On the other, there are those such as Roger Hadley and Stephen Hatch (1981) who see the solution in terms of greater decentralization, devolution, and democratization in policy-making and implementation. They argue that voluntary associations and community groups provide the best prospects for the future development of equitable forms of health provision.

137

*Marxism*

For Marxists, an analysis of state involvement in health care in Britain must begin with an analysis of capitalist social relations. In particular, it must recognize the role of the state in mediating conflict between capitalists and workers. In contrast to pluralists, who argue that the state's actions are essentially benign, Marxists point to the existence of important alliances between the state and the capitalist class. While allowing for relative autonomy between the state and owners of capital, these connections ensure that in the final instance the state is likely to act in such a way as to further the long-term interests of capital.

It should come as little surprise therefore to find that Marxist perspectives are either ambivalent or critical of state provision for health and welfare. Thus, while Vicente Navarro (1978), in his study of the origins of the NHS, identifies the importance of working-class struggle in creating the welfare state, he points to the fact that post-1948 patterns of provision did little to challenge existing social relations – either within medicine or within society at large. Indeed, writers such as James O'Connor (1973) suggest that state intervention in health and welfare may provide the minimum needed to help legitimize the inequalities created by capitalism, and thus stave off potential discontent.

Similar ideas to this have been put forward by Andrew Friend and Andy Metcalfe (1981). In contrast to pluralists, who welcomed the creation of the welfare state as a potentially liberating force, Friend and Metcalfe view events more pessimistically. They suggest that state involvement in health and welfare allows the working class to be more oppressively supervised by professionals such as teachers, social workers, and health care specialists. According to Friend and Metcalfe, the growth of the welfare state has been accompanied by a proliferation of institutions under the control of the professional middle class, whose role it is to police the attitudes and behaviour of working-class women and men.

## Activities

1 Working in groups of three or four, make a list of professions within the health and social services whose task it is to arrange and supervise the following:
- the bringing up of children
- the care of elderly people
- the behaviour of young people
- the rehabilitation of criminals

2 Discuss how far these professionals are concerned with social welfare and how far with social control. Can these two roles be separated?

It is in the work of Claus Offe that we can find one of the most developed Marxist accounts of the role of the state in health care provision. Offe (1974) identifies three key subsystems in capitalist societies: the central political administrative system, consisting of the state and welfare services; the economic system, concerned with the production and exchange of goods; and the normative and legitimation system, concerned with the reproduction of dominant values. In his view, the first of these systems is dependent on the others for finance and for loyalty. Taxation ensures that the central political administrative system remains financially secure, whereas the provision of health and welfare services helps maintain loyalty to the state. Imbalances between these systems can create crises of many kinds – some may be economic, some may be administrative, and some may be to do with legitimation. State involvement in health and welfare is usually concerned with managing these crises.

### Feminism

Like Marxist perspectives, feminist analyses tend to be critical in their stance. Many of them identify the patriarchal

139

assumptions that have underpinned state involvement in health and welfare. The Women's Social and Political Union, for example, singled out the 1911 National Insurance Act for special criticism. This discriminated against married women by offering insurance only to wage-earners.

> The fundamental principle of the Bill is not national insurance of the working class, but insurance of the wage earner, and in consequence one half of the women of the country are omitted from its provisions. This applies not only to benefit money paid during sickness but to medical attention, which will accordingly be withheld from a vast number of women. The result is to penalise the valuable work that women are doing within the home without wages, whether as wives or as daughters or sisters.
>
> (Women's Social and Political Union 1911: 794)

Similar views were expressed thirty years later about the assumptions of the Beveridge Report, which linked married women's health and welfare benefits to the insurance contributions paid by their husbands. A considerable amount of subsequent post-war legislation was also premised on the assumption that state provision should be made on the basis of 'family' units, not for the individuals within them. These arrangements were grossly unfair to women since they denied them their status as individuals, and treated them instead as the appendages of the men to whom they were married. As Elizabeth Abbott and Katherine Bompas put it:

> The error – an error which lies in the moral rather than the economic sphere – lies in denying to the married woman, rich or poor, housewife or paid worker, an independent personal status. From this error springs a crop of injustices and complications and difficulties, personal, marital and administrative.
>
> (Abbott and Bompas 1943: 3)

Feminists writing in the 1970s turned their attention to wider health issues, including the provision of adequate health and social services for women, the right to safe contraception, the right to abortion, and the right to adequate maternity and child benefits. According to Mary McIntosh, much of this concern was triggered by

> a growing awareness that women figure prominently among the clients of social workers, the inmates of geriatric and psychiatric hospitals, the claimants of supplementary benefits – despite the fact that married and co-habiting women are not eligible for many benefits.
>
> (McIntosh 1981: 32)

The 1980s have seen feminist researchers examining the distinctive nature of women's health experience, the role of women as unpaid providers of care for elderly and infirm people, and the mechanisms which ensure that in matters to do with health and welfare, women remain dependent on men. Patriarchy operates in all these areas of life: through ideologies which make it seem natural that women and men should be provided for in particular ways, through processes which govern the allocation and distribution of health resources, and through overt discrimination at the point of service delivery. In analysing the coherence of women's health experience under patriarchy, Hilary Land asks, 'Why then do the state's income maintenance schemes still only support men in the role of chief breadwinner and woman as man's dependent housewife?' For her, the answer must lie in the fact that there are

> enormous advantages to the economically most powerful groups in our society in sustaining the belief that men are breadwinners and women, at most, are supplementary earners, whose primary duties lie in the home. ... In this way ... women when they enter the labour market do so in the belief that they do not need as high a wage as a man. Moreover, their paid employment must take second place to their unpaid work at home. ... At the same time they continue to care for their husbands, children, the elderly

141

and the infirm at minimum cost to the state. However, it should not be forgotten, of course, that when we talk of economic advantages, we have, as Eleanor Rathbone pointed out forty years ago *'an economic structure devised by and for men'*.

(Land 1978: 142, emphasis added)

## Conclusions

The perspectives discussed in this chapter are not only of academic interest, but also inform the actions of politicians and policy-makers, as well as professionals working in medicine and health. Thus liberalism, pluralism, Marxism, and feminism are not simply frameworks by which to analyse *past* events; they are perspectives that lie behind the actions of women and men involved in policy-making *today*. The task of the sociologist, in making sense of modern health policy, is to identify these perspectives in action. Only by doing this can we properly understand the events that have transpired and the interests that lay behind them.

When I first began writing this book, the intention was to produce an overview of some of the key issues concerning sociologists working in the field of health and illness. Central among these were questions of definition, measurement, and explanation. Also of interest were the consequences of particular theoretical frameworks for contemporary health policy. In the space available, it has not been possible to do more than sketch out the main features of the most important debates. I hope, though, that having read this book, you will feel inspired to follow up the issues that interest you; and I hope that, having done this, you will feel more prepared to respond to the challenges that will face us all in the years ahead.

## Further reading

*Numerous books have been written on policy and practice in the health field, but many of them suffer from the problems identified on pp. 133–4, by failing to analyse the complex economic, political, and social processes that lie behind the events described. A recent book by Clarke, Cochrane, and Smart (1987) does not fall into this trap, and offers a variety of accounts of the processes contributing to particular policy decisions. Likewise, chapters 6 and 8 in Graham (1985) contain a number of readings identifying liberal, pluralist (social-democratic), Marxist, and feminist perspectives on health and welfare policy.*

# References

Abbott, E. and Bompas, K. (1943) 'The woman citizen and Social Security', London: unpublished manuscript.

Acheson, D. and Hagard, S. (1984) *Health, Society and Medicine*, Oxford: Blackwell Scientific Publications Ltd.

Aggleton, P. (1987) *Deviance*, London: Tavistock

Aggleton, P. and Homans, H. (1987) *Educating about AIDS*, Bristol: National Health Service Training Authority.

Albrecht, G.L. and Higgins, P.C. (eds) (1979) *Health, Illness and Medicine*, Chicago, Ill: Rand McNally.

Armitage, K. (1979) 'Response of physicians to medical complaints in men and women', *Journal of the American Medical Association* 241: 186–7.

Arms, S. (1975) *Immaculate Deception: A New Look at Women and Childbirth in America*, Boston, Mass: Houghton Mifflin.

Armstrong, D. (1983) *An Outline of Sociology as Applied to Medicine*, Bristol: John Wright.

Barker-Benfield, G.J. (1976) *The Horrors of the Half-Known Life*, New York: Harper Colophon Books.

Becker, H. (1963) *Outsiders: Studies in the Sociology of Deviance*, New York: Free Press.

—— (1964) *The Other Side: Perspectives on Deviance*, New York: Free Press.

Bhat, A., Carr-Hill, R., and Ohri, S. (1988) *Britain's Black Population*, Aldershot: Gower.

Bilton, T., Bonnett, K., Jones, P., Stanworth, M., Sheard, K., and Webster, A. (1987) *Introductory Sociology*, Basingstoke: Macmillan.

Black, N., Boswell, D., Gray, A., Murphy, S., and Popay, J. (eds) (1984) *Health and Disease – A Reader*, Milton Keynes: Open University Press.

Blaxter, M. (1983) 'The causes of disease: women talking', *Social Science and Medicine* 17, 2. 59–69.

—— (1987) 'Evidence on inequality in health from a national survey', *Lancet* ii: 30–3.

Blaxter, M. and Paterson, E. (1982) *Mothers and Daughters: A Three-Generational Study of Health Attitudes and Health Behaviour*, London: Heinemann.

Blumer, H. (1969) *Symbolic Interactionism*, Berkeley, CA: University of California Press.

Boyd, C. and Sellars, L. (1982) *The British Way of Birth*, London: Spastics International Medical Publications.

Byrne, P. and Long, B. (1976) *Doctors Talking to Patients*, London: HMSO.

Calnan, M. (1987) *Health and Illness – The Lay Perspective*, London: Tavistock.

Cartwright, A. (1967) *Patients and their Doctors*, London: Routledge & Kegan Paul.

Central Office of Information (1989) *Britain – An Official Handbook*, London: HMSO.

Central Statistical Office (1986) *Social Trends, 16*, London: HMSO.

Clarke, J., Cochrane, A., and Smart, C. (1987) *Ideologies of Welfare*, London: Hutchinson.

Collier, J. (1989) *The Health Conspiracy*, London: Century Books.

Connerton, P. (1976) *Critical Sociology*, Harmondsworth: Penguin.

Conrad, P. and Schneider, J. (1980) *Deviance and Medicalization*, St Louis, Missouri: Mosby.

Cooley, C. (1909) *Human Nature and the Social Order*, Glencoe, Ill: Free Press.

Cooper, D. (1971) *The Death of the Family*, London: Allen Lane.

Cornwell, J. (1984) *Hard Earned Lives – Accounts of Health and Illness from East London*, London: Tavistock.

Coulthard, M. and Ashby, M. (1976) 'A linguistic description of doctor-patient interviews', in M. Wadsworth and D. Robinson (eds) *Studies in Everyday Medical Life*, Oxford: Martin Robertson.

Cox, B. (1987) 'Health and Life-style Survey Preliminary Report', Cambridge: Health Promotion Trust.

Currer, C. and Stacey, M. (eds) (1986) *Concepts of Health, Illness and Disease*, Leamington Spa: Berg.

Daly, M. (1979) *Gyn/Ecology: the metaethics of feminism*, London: The Women's Press.

Denzin, N. (1987) *The Alcoholic Self*, Beverly Hills, CA: Sage.

Doll, R. and Peto, R. (1976) 'Mortality in relation to smoking: 20 years observation on male British doctors', *British Medical Journal* 2: 1525–36.

Donovan, J. (1984) 'Ethnicity and health: a research review', *Social Science and Medicine* 19, 7: 663–70.

Doyal, L. and Pennell, I. (1979) *The Political Economy of Health*, London: Pluto Press.

Dubos, R. (1959) *The Mirage of Health*, New York: Harper & Row.

Durkheim, E. (1966) *Rules of Sociological Method*, New York: Free Press.

Durkheim, E. (1970) *Suicide*, London: Routledge & Kegan Paul.

Durant, W. and Durant, A. (1952) *The Story of Civilisation: 1 Our Indian Heritage*, New York: Simon & Schuster.

Ehrenreich, B. and English, D. (1973) *Witches, Midwives and Nurses*, New York: Feminist Press.

—— (1978) *For Her Own Good: A Hundred and Fifty Years of the Experts's Advice to Women*, New York: Anchor Press.

Ewles, L. and Simnett, I. (1985) *Promoting Health: A Practical Guide to Health Education*, Chichester: John Wiley.

Fennell, G., Phillipson, C., and Evers, H. (1988) *The Sociology of Old Age*, Milton Keynes: Open University Press.

Field, D. (1976) 'The social definition of illness', in D. Tuckett (ed.) *An Introduction to Medical Sociology*, London: Tavistock.

Fitzpatrick, R. (1984) 'Lay concepts of illness', in R. Fitzpatrick, J. Hinton, S. Newman, G. Scambler, and J. Thompson (eds) *The Experience of Illness*, London: Tavistock.

Fitzpatrick, R., Hinton, J., Newman, S., Scambler, G., and Thompson, J. (eds) (1984) *The Experience of Illness*, London: Tavistock.

Ford, J. (1976) 'Clinical and sub-clinical Vitamin D deficiency in Bradford children', *Lancet* i: 1,141.

Foster, G. (1983) 'An introduction to ethnomedicine', in R. Bannerman, J. Burton, and C. Wen-Chieh (eds) *Traditional Medicine and Health Coverage*, Geneva: World Health Organisation.

Foucault, M. (1974) *The Birth of the Clinic: An Archaeology of Medical Perception*, London: Tavistock.

Freidson, E. (1970) *Profession of Medicine*, New York: Dodd Mead.

—— (1988) *Profession of Medicine*, 2nd edn, Chicago, Ill: Chicago University Press.

Friedman, M. and Friedman, R. (1980) *Free to Choose*, London: Secker & Warburg.

Friend, A. and Metcalfe, A. (1981) *Slump City*, London: Pluto Press.

Giel, R. and Van Luijk, J. (1970) 'Leprosy in Ethiopian society', *International Journal of Leprosy* 38: 187–94.

Goel, K. (1976) 'Florid and sub-clinical rickets amongst immigrant children in Glasgow', *Archives of Disease in Childhood* 17: 939.

Goffman, E. (1959) *The Presentation of the Self in Everyday Life*, New York: Doubleday.

—— (1963) *Stigma: Notes on the Management of Spoiled Identity*, Harmondsworth: Penguin.

—— (1968) *Asylums*, Harmondsworth: Penguin.

Goldthorpe, J., Lockwood, D., Bechoffer, F., and Platt, J. (1969) *The Affluent Worker in the Class Structure*, Cambridge: Cambridge University Press.

Goode, E. (1984) *Deviant Behaviour*, Englewood Cliffs, NJ: Prentice-Hall.

Graham, H. (1985) *Health and Welfare*, Basingstoke: Macmillan.

Green, D. (1987) *The New Right*, Brighton: Wheatsheaf.

Gregory, J. (1978) 'Patients' attitudes to the hospital service – a survey carried out for the Royal Commission on the National Health Service', Res. Paper no. 5, London: HMSO.

Griffith, B., Iliffe, S., and Rayner, G. (1987) *Banking on Sickness*, London: Lawrence & Wishart.

Grimsley, M. and Bhat, A. (1988) 'Health', in A. Bhat, R. Carr-Hill, and S. Ohri (eds) *Britain's Black Population*, Aldershot: Gower.

Hadley, R. and Hatch, S. (1981) *Social Welfare and the Failure of the State*, London: Allen & Unwin.

Ham, C. (1985) *Health Policy in Britain*, Basingstoke: Macmillan.

Hart, N. (1985) *The Sociology of Health and Medicine*, Ormskirk: Causeway Press.

Hartmann, H. (1981) 'The unhappy marriage of Marxism and

feminism', in H. Hartmann and L. Sargent, *The Unhappy Marriage of Marxism and Feminism*, London: Pluto Press.

Hartmann, H. and Sargent, L. (1981) *The Unhappy Marriage of Marxism and Feminism*, London: Pluto Press.

Helman, C. (1978) '"Feed a cold, starve a fever": Folk models of infection in an English suburban community and their relation to medical treatment', *Culture, Medicine and Society* 2: 107–37.

Herzlich, C. (1973) *Health and Illness: A Social Psychological Analysis*, London: Academic Press.

Homans, H. (ed.) (1986) *The Sexual Politics of Reproduction*, Aldershot: Gower.

House of Commons (1988) *Perinatal, Neonatal and Infant Mortality*, HC Paper 54, London: HMSO.

Hunt, A. (1978) *The Elderly at Home: A Study of People aged 65 and Over Living in the Community in England in 1976*, London: HMSO.

Illich, I. (1975) *Limits to Medicine*, Harmondsworth: Penguin.

Jewson, N. (1976) 'The disappearance of the sick man from medical cosmology, 1770–1870', *Sociology* 10, 2: 225–44.

Johnson, B. (1975) 'Righteousness before revenue: the forgotten moral crusade against the Indo-Chinese opium trade', *Journal of Drug Issues* 5: 304–26.

Jones, K. and Moon, G. (1987) *Health, Disease and Society*, London: Routledge & Kegan Paul.

Kleinman, A. (1980) *Patients and Healers in the Context of Culture*, Berkeley, CA: University of California Press.

Krieger, D. (1981) *Foundations for Holistic Health Nursing Practices*, Philadelphia, Pa: Lippincott.

Laing, R.D. (1961) *Self and Others*, London: Tavistock.

Laing, R.D. and Esterson, A. (1964) *Sanity, Madness and the Family*, London: Tavistock.

Land, H. (1978) 'Sex role stereotyping in the social security and income tax systems', in J. Chetwynd and O. Hartnett (eds) *The Sex Role System*, London: Routledge & Kegan Paul.

Laws, S. (1985) 'Male power and menstrual etiquette', in H. Homans (ed.) *The Sexual Politics of Reproduction*, Aldershot: Gower.

Lemert, E. (1967) *Human Deviance, Social Problems and Social Control*, Englewood Cliffs, NJ: Prentice-Hall.

Lerner, H. (1974) 'The hysterical personality – a woman's disease', *Comprehensive Psychiatry* 15: 157–64.

Lindesmith, A.R. (1947) *Opiate Addiction*, Bloomington, Ind: Principia Press.

—— (1968) *Addiction and Opiates*, Chicago, Ill: Aldine.

Lorber, J. (1984) *Women Physicians*, London: Tavistock.

MacFarlane, A. and Mugford, M. (1984) *Birth Counts: Statistics of Pregnancy and Childbirth*, London: HMSO.

McIntosh, M. (1981) 'Feminism and social policy', *Critical Social Policy* 1:1.

Macintyre, S. (1986) 'Health and Illness', in R. Burgess (ed.) *Key Variables in Social Investigation*, London: Routledge & Kegan Paul.

Macintyre, S. and Oldman, D. (1984) 'Coping with migraine' in N Black, D. Boswell, A. Gray, S. Murphy, and J. Popay (eds) *Health and Disease: A Reader*, Milton Keynes: Open University Press.

McKeown, T. (1976) *The Modern Rise of Population*, London: Edward Arnold.

—— (1979) *The Role of Medicine: Dream, Mirage or Nemesis?* Oxford: Basil Blackwell.

McKinley, J. (1977) 'The business of good doctoring or doctoring as good business: reflections of Freidson's view of the medical game', *International Journal of Health Services* 7, 3: 459–83.

Marmot, M., Adelstein, A., and Balusu, L. (1984) 'Immigrant mortality in England and Wales 1970–78', *OPCS Studies on Medical and Population Subjects*, No. 47, London: HMSO.

Marx, K. (1976) *Capital, Volume 1*, Harmondsworth: Penguin.

Mead, G.H. (1934) 'Mind, self and society', in C. Morris (ed.) *Mind, Self and Society*, Chicago, Ill: University of Chicago Press.

Mechanic, D. (1978) *Medical Sociology: A Comprehensive Text*, New York: Free Press.

Melrose, D. (1982) *Bitter Pills – Medicines and the Third World Poor*, Oxford: Oxfam.

Mishler, E., Amarasingham, L.R., Hauser, S.T., Liem, R., Osherson, S.D., and Waxler, N. (1981) *Social Contexts of Health, Illness and Patient Care*, Cambridge: Cambridge University Press.

Mitchell, J. (1984) *What is to be Done about Illness and Health?*, Harmondsworth: Penguin.

Navarro, V. (1976) *Medicine under Capitalism*, New York: Prodist.

—— (1978) *Class Struggle, the State and Medicine*, Oxford: Martin Robertson.

Oakley, A. (1979) 'The trap of medicalized motherhood', in Bristol Women's Studies Group, *Half the Sky*, London: Virago.

—— (1980) *Women Confined*, Oxford: Martin Robertson.

—— (1984) *The Captured Womb: A History of the Medical Care of Pregnant Women*, Oxford: Basil Blackwell.

O'Connor, J. (1973) *The Fiscal Crisis of the State*, New York: St Martin's Press.

Offe, C. (1974) 'Structural problems of the capitalist state', in K. Von Beyme (ed.) *German Political Studies, Volume 1*, Beverly Hills, CA: Sage.

—— (1975) 'The theory of the capitalist state and the problem of policy formation' in L. Lindberg, R. Alford, C. Crouch, and C. Offe (eds) *Stress and Contradiction in Modern Capitalism*, London: Lexington Books.

OPCS (1978) *Occupational Mortality: 1970–2*, London: HMSO.

—— (1982) *Mortality Statistics, England and Wales, 1982*, Series DH2, no. 9, London: HMSO.

—— (1983) *Occupational Mortality, decennial supplement 1979–83*; Series DS, no. 6, London: HMSO.

—— (1984) *Mortality Statistics, Perinatal and Infant: Social and Biological Factors for 1984*, Series DH3, no. 17, London: HMSO.

—— (1985) *General Household Survey for 1983*, London: HMSO.

—— (1986) *General Household Survey for 1984*, London: HMSO.

Open University (1985a) *Studying Health and Disease*, Book 1 of *Health and Disease* (U205), Milton Keynes: Open University Press.

—— (1985b) *Medical Knowledge: Doubt and Certainty*, Book 2 of *Health and Disease* (U205), Milton Keynes: Open University Press.

—— (1985c) *The Health of Nations*, Book 3 of *Health and Disease* (U205), Milton Keynes: Open University Press.

Parker, H., Bakx, K., and Newcombe, R. (1988) *Living with Heroin*, Milton Keynes: Open University Press.

Parsons, T. (1951) *The Social System*, Glencoe, Ill: Free Press.

—— (1972) 'Definitions of health and illness in the light of American values and social structure', in E. Jaco and E. Gartley (eds) *Patients, Physicians and Illness: A Sourcebook in Behavioural Science and Health*, London: Collier-Macmillan.

Pearson, G., Gilman, M., and McIver, S. (1985) *Young People and Heroin*, Research Report no. 8, London: Health Education Council.

Penfold, P.S. and Walker, G. (1984) *Women and the Psychiatric Paradox*, Milton Keynes: Open University Press.

150

Pfeffer, N. (1985) 'The hidden pathology of the male reproductive system', in H. Homans (ed.) *The Sexual Politics of Reproduction*, Aldershot: Gower.

Pollock, S. (1985) 'Sex and the contraceptive act', in H. Homans (ed.) *The Sexual Politics of Reproduction*, Aldershot: Gower.

Popkin, A. (1979) 'The personal is political: the women's liberation movement', in D. Cluster (ed.) *They Should Have Served that Cup of Coffee*, Boston, Mass: South End Press.

Ray, O. (1978) *Drugs, Society and Human Behaviour*, St Louis, Missouri: Mosby.

Rich, A. (1972) *Of Woman Born: Motherhood as Experience and Institution*, New York: Norton.

Rose, G. and Marmot, M (1981) 'Social class and coronary heart disease', *British Medical Journal* 45: 13–19.

Rosenhan, D. (1973) 'On being sane in insane places', *Science* 179: 250–8.

Roth, J. (1972) 'Some contingencies of the moral evaluation and control of clientele: the case of the hospital emergency service', *American Journal of Sociology* 77: 839–56.

Sacks, O. (1982) *Awakenings*, London: Pan.

Scott, J.M. (1969) *The White Poppy*, New York: Harper & Row.

Seedhouse, D. (1986) *Health: The Foundations for Achievement*, Chichester: John Wiley.

Showalter, E. (1987) *The Female Malady: Women, Madness and English Culture, 1830–1980*, London: Virago.

Spitzer, S. and Denzin, N. (1968) *The Mental Patient – Studies in the Sociology of Deviance*, New York: McGraw Hill.

Stacey, M. (1988) *The Sociology of Health and Healing*, London: Unwin Hyman.

Summers, M. (1971) *The Malleus Maleficarum of Heinrich Kramer and James Sprenger*, New York: Dover Publications.

Taylor, S. (1987) *Suicide*, London: Longman.

Thomas, K. (1971) *Religion and the Decline of Magic*, London: Weidenfeld & Nicolson.

Thomas, W. (1923) *The Unadjusted Girl*, Boston, Mass: Little, Brown.

Titmuss, R. (1970) *The Gift Relationship*, Harmondsworth: Penguin.

Townsend, P. (1984) *Why are the Many Poor?*, London: Fabian Society.

Townsend, P. and Davidson, N. (1982) *Inequalities in Health*, Harmondsworth: Penguin.

Townsend, P., Davidson, N., and Whitehead, M. (1988) *Inequalities in Health and The Health Divide*, Harmondsworth: Penguin.

Tuckett, D. (1976) 'Work, life-chances and life-styles', in D. Tuckett (ed.) *An Introduction to Medical Sociology*, London: Tavistock.

Turner, B. (1982) 'The government of the body: medical regimens and the rationalization of diet', *British Journal of Sociology* 33, 2: 25–69.

—— (1987) *Medical Power and Social Knowledge*, Beverly Hills, CA: Sage.

United Nations (1981) *Demographic Yearbook*, New York: United Nations.

Unschuld, P. (1986) 'The conceptual determination (*Uberformung*) of individual and collective experiences of health', in C. Currer and M. Stacey (eds) *Concepts of Health, Illness and Disease*, Leamington Spa: Berg.

Victor, C. (1987) *Old Age in Modern Society*, London: Croom Helm.

Waddington, I. (1973) 'The role of hospitals in the development of modern medicine: a sociological analysis', *Sociology* 7: 211–24.

Wadsworth, M. (1986) 'Serious illness in childhood and its association with later-life achievement', in R.G. Wilkinson (ed.) *Class and Health: Research and Longitudinal Data*, London: Tavistock.

Wadsworth, M. and Robinson, D. (1976) *Studies in Everyday Medical Life*, Oxford: Martin Robertson.

Waitzkin, H. and Waterman, B. (1974) *The Exploitation of Illness in Capitalist Society*, Indianapolis, Ind: Bobbs-Merrill.

Warwick, I., Aggleton, P., and Homans, H. (1988) 'Constructing commonsense – young people's beliefs about AIDS', *Sociology of Health and Illness* 10, 3: 213–33.

Watkins, S. (1987) *Medicine and Labour*, London: Lawrence & Wishart.

Waxler, N. (1981) 'Learning to be a leper', in E. Mishler, L. Amarasingham, S. Hauser, R. Liem, S. Osherson, and N. Waxler *Social Contexts of Health, Illness and Patient Care*, Cambridge: Cambridge University Press.

Welbourne, J. and Purgold, J. (1984) *The Eating Sickness – Anorexia, Bulimia and the Myth of Suicide by Slimming*, Brighton: Harvester.

WHO (1946) *Constitution*, Geneva: World Health Organisation.

Williams, R. (1983) 'Concepts of health: an analysis of lay logic', *Sociology* 17, 2: 185–205.

Willmott, P. and Young, M. (1962) *Family and Class in a London Suburb*, London: Routledge & Kegan Paul.

Women's Social and Political Union (1911) *Votes for Women*, 15 September: 794.

Young, M. and Willmott, P. (1973) *The Symmetrical Family*, Harmondsworth: Penguin.

# Index